# SURVIVAL WITHIN
# TWO CULTURES

# SURVIVAL WITHIN TWO CULTURES

## A Memoir

**ERMINIA "MINNIE" LOPEZ RINCON**

iUniverse, Inc.
Bloomington

**Survival Within Two Cultures**
**A Memoir**

Copyright © 2012 by Erminia "Minnie" Lopez Rincon

All rights reserved. No part of this book may be used or reproduced by any means, graphic, electronic, or mechanical, including photocopying, recording, taping or by any information storage retrieval system without the written permission of the publisher except in the case of brief quotations embodied in critical articles and reviews.

iUniverse books may be ordered through booksellers or by contacting:

iUniverse
1663 Liberty Drive
Bloomington, IN 47403
www.iuniverse.com
1-800-Authors (1-800-288-4677)

Because of the dynamic nature of the Internet, any web addresses or links contained in this book may have changed since publication and may no longer be valid. The views expressed in this work are solely those of the author and do not necessarily reflect the views of the publisher, and the publisher hereby disclaims any responsibility for them.

Any people depicted in stock imagery provided by Thinkstock are models, and such images are being used for illustrative purposes only.

Certain stock imagery © Thinkstock.

ISBN: 978-1-4620-7313-9 (sc)
ISBN: 978-1-4620-7314-6 (hc)
ISBN: 978-1-4620-7315-3 (e)

Library of Congress Control Number: 2011962417

Printed in the United States of America

iUniverse rev. date: 12/29/2011

For my children, Mark, Marcie, Judy, and Wendy,
and *survivors*.

# Contents

Introduction ........................................... 1

I. Early Years ..................................... 4

II. Mother's Death, Repercussions .................. 22

III. Elementary and High School Experience ........... 30

IV. Sister Elopes, Sexual Molestation, Father Marries ..... 38

V. Graduation / Seeking Employment ................ 47

VI. Dating ........................................ 54

VII. Marriage, Children, Discrimination ............... 63

VIII. Overload, Splitting Sensations, Therapy ........... 89

IX. Dream Realized—College ...................... 103

X. Spain/France Trip, Purdue BS, and Mentor Help .... 106

XI. Lopez Brothers' Death, Temporary Employment, Marriage .................................... 117

XII. Graduate Student of University of Illinois, Publications, Mentor's Death ................... 123

XIII. Rudy's Trip, Divorce .......................... 127

XIV. Old Molestation Issue Surfaces, Temporary Employment .................................. 130

XV. Employment, Family Wedding .................. 138

XVI. School Psychologist, Sexual Abuse ............... 142

XVII. Professional Embarrassment .................... 156

| XVIII. | Rudy's Death / Death of Son | 168 |
| --- | --- | --- |
| XIX. | Retirement and Self-Employment | 185 |
| XX. | End of Twenty-Five-Year Friendship | 199 |
| XXI. | Correcting an Omission | 205 |
| XXII. | Financial Loss | 214 |

# Acknowledgment

Profuse thanks to Lupe and Barb for editing this manuscript, for saving this inept Internet user from giving up. Thanks to daughters Marcie, Wendy, and Judy and friends Barb and Jeff, who did not abandon me, and Mary B. for her help with family background.

# Introduction

For many years I have been toying with the notion of writing about my life—the early years, the middle, and the present. But where does one begin? Perhaps I can begin by noting that I would not be in this country writing my memoirs had it not been for the courage and drive of my father and his two brothers to defy conscription into the Mexican Revolutionary Army. Death and brutal behavior inflicted on the families were the penalties for not supporting the revolution. To avoid these dire consequences, in 1918 the Lopez brothers gathered their families and left their homes in San Luis Potosi and began the arduous trek northward to Texas and safety. One can surmise that starting anew in a strange country and not being adept in the language spoken was not an easy undertaking.

With the foregoing as background, I offer that this manuscript is about my struggle as an American/Mexican female to rise above my humble beginnings in a railroad camp and then suffer the restrictions and discrimination faced because of my ethnic background. Other crucial issues are the aftermath of losing mother figures at a very young age and the physical and financial raping to which I was subjected by individuals whom I trusted. The values of honesty, trustworthiness, and charity I learned from the overt behavior of the Lopez brothers, and their wives were not those espoused by some unscrupulous individuals with whom I came into contact. These are issues that should not only be of interest to those who have had similar experiences but also to professionals involved in the psychological and sociological realms. My burning desire for a college education is unique because in the 1960s, less than 1 percent of the Hispanic population was enrolled in a college or university. Further, education beyond grade school and possibly high school was not considered necessary or appropriate for Hispanic females. Three professionals—because of their positive comments about my writing ability—were instrumental in giving me the confidence to undertake this task: an English teacher, a college professor, and an editor who received one of my manuscripts

Compartmentalizing eighty-plus years is a challenging feat. First, one could start by stating, "I was born." Big deal—wasn't everybody who lived? However, relatives and friends who lived in the camp related that I was not breathing at birth. The attendant working on me did not give up until I was breathing. Those who knew this are dead; hence, I cannot verify whether the foregoing is true. There is a question also about my name. When my father was upset with me, he called me Erminia and, when not upset, Mine. The latter is pronounced with a soft *e* at the end, like the *e* in bed. Through grade school and high school, I was known as Minnie. When looking up records prior to marriage, I found that on my birth certificate my name was registered as Minnie Lopez. On the baptismal record, it is "Erminia." I reasoned that the clerk who registered my birth was unfamiliar with the Spanish name "Erminia" and translated it as "Minnie." I cannot explain why I resorted to the name "Erminia" when I was married, on college forms, and on employment and other documents. When there is a question about my names, the explanation given is accepted. Except when absolutely necessary, I prefer the name "Minnie."

At the time of my birth, my family consisted of a father, a mother, two older brothers, and four sisters. Two years after my birth, my mother gave birth to a daughter and, two years later, gave birth to a stillborn child, a female. The incidents reported do not always follow each other chronologically because one incident may be better understood when presented as a whole—that is, with background prior it.

# 1

My father and his two brothers were born in San Luis Potosi, Mexico. Occasionally I overheard my father mention that his and his brothers' families fled Mexico in 1918 because the brothers refused to join the revolutionary army. Because of their adamant refusal, they feared severe consequences, which included execution. Further, the female members would suffer indignities at the hands of the soldiers. Recently, Uncle Manuel's daughter, Mary Bustamante, shared with me the information her mother told her children. Manuel never talked about the flight from Mexico. He vowed he would never return and he did not! Mary related that one evening Manuel and Luis became aware that they were being watched. Fearing that they would be attacked, they fled home and prepared to leave Mexico. No time was lost gathering their families, including Benito's. With the few possessions and supplies that could be carried, they left their homes and headed for the United States border. A rough estimate of the mileage from San Luis Potosi to Eagle Pass, Texas, is 576 miles. It was an incredibly dangerous trek through rough terrain—often through undeveloped land. Information as to how the families made it to the border is not available. All involved in the escape are deceased. The families entered the United States legally via Eagle Pass, Texas, in 1918. The only entry permits that were found are those of my aunt Silveria and uncle Manuel. These are shown below. My sister Trini was born in Texas on September 21, 1920.

At the time of their entry, Uncle Manuel and his wife, Silveria, had three sons, Calixto, John, and Erie, and one daughter, Mary. My father and his wife, Ildefonsa, entered the United States with two sons, Walter and Joseph, and two daughters, Cecilia and Joan.

Uncle Benito and Bascilia, his wife, had three sons, Lino, Angel, and Boniface. Angel returned to Mexico and subsequently entered the seminary. He was ordained on June 3, 1939, and died on July 24, 2009, at the age of ninety-six. Bascilia died in Texas. Details are unknown. Subsequently, Benito, leaving his sons with Aunt Silveria, returned to Mexico to marry Cenobia, the daughter of a family whom he knew in Mexico. The newly married couple returned to Texas and were reunited with their sons. Manuel and his oldest son, Calixto, found work on the railroad. The joy of finding work with the railroad was marred by Mary's death. While in her brother John's care, she strayed from him and was struck and killed by a freight train. She was five years of age. It is not known whether her death prompted the family to relocate to Dallas. In March of 1921, Silveria gave birth to a daughter, whom they named Paula. Benito and Luis, along with the older children found work on the farms.

Subsequently, the three Lopez brothers left Texas with their families and headed north and eastward in search of employment that would provide a better living for their families. Manuel, Silveria, three sons, and daughter settled in Kansas City, Missouri, where Mary was born. Mary was named after the sister who was killed by the freight train. The first home for the family was a rented apartment on Monitor Street, which was over a grocery store and a barbershop. I recall visiting the family then and the fun my sisters and our cousins had in that apartment. We could crawl out the window of one of the rooms and step onto the roof of the barbershop. Playfully, we would get small soft pebbles, and as their patrons left the shop, we would try to hit their heads. When they looked up, of course, they were not able to see us, as we had scooted away from the edge of the roof. Another episode that remains vivid in my mind may have taken place at a subsequent apartment. When we misbehaved, Aunt

Silveria would take a broom and chase us as we ran around the large round table in the dining room. While she chased us, her face would break into a smile, which she tried to hide, and we ended up laughing. Uncle Manuel bought houses first on Holly Street and then bought one on Pennsylvania Street. In 1967 he bought a home on Washington Street, where the family lived until his death. Aunt Silveria's death followed one year later. Mary Bustamante, their youngest child, raised her children in her parents' house, and it continues to be her home.

Uncle Manuel was hired by the Frisco Railroad, remaining in their employ until he was forced into an early retirement at the age of fifty-eight. He was struck by a bus and injured so severely that he was in danger of losing his leg. He was adamant that he would not allow his leg to be amputated. It was through prayer by all and sheer will that he kept his leg. However, he was no longer able to work. Once, he showed me the damage done to his leg. It was not a pretty sight. His determination and courage to keep his leg to maintain his mobility was remarkable. He walked on his two legs, wearing two shoes, to the end of his life on December 24, 1973, at eighty-six years of age.

Benito and Cenobia and their sons, Lino and Boniface, traveled north to Fort Worth, Texas. While in Texas, Leonard and Martin were born. Sometime later, they continued north and then west to McIntyre, Michigan, where Cenobia gave birth to a daughter, Pat. I can only surmise that Benito wished to locate to the Chicago, Illinois area to be near his brother Luis, who had made his home in Blue Island, Illinois. An apartment was found on Bishop Street, and there, Lupe was born. The family then relocated to an English apartment on Wallace Street, near 119th Street. Subsequently Joey, Sabina, and Bob were born. Bishop and Wallace streets are at the southern outskirts of Chicago and near Blue Island's northern boundary. The next move for the family was to Grove Street in Blue Island, where Mary was born. Martin had died on August 5, 1926, due to complications from a childhood illness. He was four and a half years old. He was buried in Blue Island, Illinois.

In time, Uncle Benito and his family returned to Chicago, to an area west of Grant Park and the museums. Benito found employment at the International Harvester Co. and left there in April of 1929 to work for the Chicago Malleable Casket Co. until his retirement. Uncle Benito and my father visited frequently. However, that is not to say that Uncle Manuel was ignored. Though infrequent, the brothers visited each other occasionally and made an effort to visit whenever there was need. Furthermore, writing was not a skill the brothers lacked, and communication was carried on via the mail. And their penmanship, word usage, and language were very well developed. I recall that Aunt Silveria, Uncle Manuel's wife, too, wrote to my father and to Uncle Benito. Visits and words between the brothers may have been few, but one need only observe the three brothers together to sense the closeness and esteem they had for each other. I recall visiting my relatives in Kansas City after the death of my father in 1971. Because Uncle Manuel was not in good health, he had not been told of his brother's death. When I appeared before him, he looked at me sadly and said, "Se acabo mi hermano" (My brother is finished, ended, has died), and nothing else.

# 2

When Uncle Benito and Aunt Cenobia's family's moved to Blue Island, the cousins met frequently. When they relocated to the west side of Chicago, interaction became infrequent until my sisters and I were in our teens and became adept at using public transportation. We spent many weekends at my aunt and uncle's home in Chicago, a great city in which to have fun with our cousins, Pat, Leonard, and Lupe. Up and down, Maxwell (east/west axis) and Halsted (north/south axis) vendors set up shop on the sidewalks, often in front of theirs or other's retail stores and sometimes in the streets. The area presented a flea market atmosphere. It was enjoyable to spend Sundays, or any day, walking up and down these streets to browse and examine the variety of and unusual wares the merchants brought to the area. It was an area where it would be wise to consider the caveat "buyer beware" because one could be fleeced. Generally, we had no intention of buying anything. Looking cost us nothing, if we ignored the pressure by the vendors insisting we buy their product.

When I worked at an insurance company in the 1940s, I mentioned the area as being interesting; one of my coworkers asked me to take her there. So on a sunday, we took off for Maxwell Street. My friend was intrigued by the activity of the area. The area teemed with locals and visitors to Chicago. We browsed the area and looked over the myriad of unusual articles, clothing, foods, etc. As I recall, after haggling over the price with a vendor, we each bought a package of one dozen pairs of nylons—cheap! The next day, Monday, we appeared at the office with our purchases to show the office staff. Proudly, we opened the packages; and as we pulled out the stockings, to our dismay, the stockings were not equal in length. Of course, the staff laughed, and we joined in the laughter. We were flabbergasted and disappointed because we had been proud of the "good" deal we had made. My friend never returned to Maxwell Street, the name by which the area was known.

Grant Park and the museums were a few miles away and within walking distance of my uncle Benito's home. I do not recall that we ever entered the museums. We preferred to walk behind them on the huge rocks that separated the museums from Lake Michigan. On Saturday evenings, the cousins would not miss dancing at the Ashland Auditorium. Generally, during summer, Sundays were spent at Grant Park, where we watched the boys play baseball.

Because of the distance, contacts or visits with the Kansas City relatives were limited. However, during summer vacation, after our mother's death, my father would have someone drive his children to the Union Station in Chicago, where we would board the Rock Island train to Kansas City, Missouri. Being with my aunt and uncle gave my sisters and I much-needed stability, and it was a joy to play and interact with our cousins. I recall my uncle Manuel greeting us and saying proudly, with an accent, "I speak English." Despite their family of five, my aunt and uncle made room for Luis's five daughters and, to my recollection, never made us feel that we were a burden.

I have fond memories of the time we spent with my father's brothers' families. And then, we grew up and started our own families, and visitations between us were rare. However, I still have the memories and cherish having had relatives to whom we could relate. Most important they provided us with experiences far beyond the limitations of the "camp" and the garbage dump!

# 3

Luis and Ildefonsa settled in Blue Island, where their family increased by three daughters. Mary was the sixth child and the first to be born in Blue Island, Illinois. Minnie was the seventh, Marge the eighth, and two years later, our mother died while giving birth to a stillborn daughter. Our father worked for the Rock Island Railroad, retiring at the age of seventy-five. He lived in Blue Island until he died at the age of eighty-four. To my recollection, our father was not beset with health problems, and if he did feel ill, he never let on or complained. He was stoical, calm, and unflinching when under stress or beset by some trauma, traits that were shared by the three brothers.

A major perk from working for the Rock Island Railroad was that housing was provided for its workers. They and their families lived in the camp. This camp was located on 123$^{rd}$ Street, about four blocks south of the Chicago city limits, bounded on the north by the Blue Island City Dump, on the south by the stockyard's feeding corrals/pens and the Rock Island Terminal, where engines and railroad cars were repaired and serviced. On the west boundary were the Rock Island rails and train depot, which provided transportation to Chicago.

The east boundary consisted of more railroads and, beyond them, another area that was home to a few Mexican families. There, to my recollection, the housing was rough and shack like in appearance.

The camp housing seemed to be put together by railroad freight cars that had been remade so that the outside and the inside hid the real identity of our home. Each boxcar was divided into four small rooms, which accommodated the ten persons in our family. The front units were connected to the back units by a roof and a wooden platform, which, in today's terms, could be termed a patio. The latter may have been about a twelve-by-twelve-feet area. It provided a play and gathering area for the kids on rainy or snow days. Not far from the boxcars, another large family lived in a large shack, floored with packed dirt. Later, before our mother's death, my oldest sister married and obtained separate housing nearby. To my recollection, six of the units housed about eight people, one four, and another was inhabited by a bachelor of Italian background. The latter seldom interacted with the residents. A rough estimate of the area of the camp, not counting the stockyard pens/corrals and the railroad roundhouse, is that it was about one square mile. East of our camp and beyond another set railroad tracks, another group of immigrants lived in shacks built of wood with dirt-packed floors. There, too, the families were large. One of the families was related to our next-door neighbor. The adult female in this house had a natural skill in nursing and cared for the sick in the two camps. She was proficient at massage, mending sprains, and healing physical ills, such as stomach problems. Between the two areas was a "clay hole" that held/collected water and was often used by the boys for swimming at their risk.

The houses lacked electricity, indoor water supply, and toilet facilities. Kerosene lamps provided lighting. We were fortunate, however, in having an outside community toilet, with running water in a tank and a chain to release it. It was in an ample room about nine by nine feet, or perhaps larger. The room had one window, about two by two feet, no curtain, and had an electric light bulb at the ceiling that provided light. The toilet facility was located some distance from the homes and kept clean by the residents. Although safety was not generally an issue, it was not pleasant to make the trip to it at night. Eventually, electricity was installed in the homes. The residents shared a community pump, where the residents drew water for their overall use. The kitchens had large cast-iron coal/wood burning stoves that provided heat, as well as the facility for cooking and heating water for bathing and other uses. To bathe, residents heated the water and then poured it into a large metal tub. The first one in the tub had the luxury of bathing in clean water, and there was a scramble to be the first. As I think back to our large family and the small quarters, it is amazing that we managed to maintain individual privacy. I do not remember ever seeing our father, my sisters, or brothers nude or half dressed. Nonetheless, families were close-knit and relied upon each other.

An older cousin, Uncle Benito's son Lino, took it upon himself to set up a school to teach the youth and installed a small library in the camp for the residents' use. As an adult, I was impressed with his command of the English vocabulary and its usage. I do not know where he was able to obtain the books, many of which were among the classics, for example, Tolstoy's *Anna Karenina*, John Milton's *Paradise Lost*, and so forth. I still have a few of the books in my possession. Milton's book is one that I have resisted reading. Throughout the years it has been in my possession, I have looked at it, opened it, closed it, and put it back on the shelf. It has bothered me that I have not been able to or not allowed myself to read it. As I write about this, it is possible that, at a subconscious level, I related the title to the loss of my mother.

It was July 18, 2011, and I was prepared to reread my manuscript one more time. Before doing that, I felt compelled to look through the current issue of a monthly periodical. As I turned the pages, my glance fell on the picture of an author, James Allen, who was being featured. Something about his countenance and deep-set eyes gave this reader a sense of his feelings and character. I could not pinpoint exactly why I was driven to read about this individual. Nonetheless, the minute the title of his masterpiece, *As a Man Thinketh*, was cited, I felt remorse that I had not thought to mention how this awesome author's book affected me.

James Allen and his masterpiece came into my life during the time I was in therapy to help me come to terms with past issues. In 1968 or somewhat later, I was in a bookstore browsing the spiritual or self-help section when a title, *As a Man Thinketh*, printed in 1968, caught my attention. It would be an awesome task to extrapolate certain excerpts from the book because every page is rife with understandable truths, in my opinion, to assist the reader in managing his or her life. At the time I bought the book, I believe I was in a power/control struggle with my therapist. After reading it, I bought a copy of the book as a gift for my *supportive* therapist.

When I bought the book in 1968, I believed it had been written during that time. I was surprised this year to learn that his book was written in 1903, when Allen was an unknown English author. His life was not one of comfort and ease. It is my misfortune that I did not explore the life of this author, who wrote extensively until his death in 1912, at which time he was forty-seven years old. I intend to correct this omission.

While on the subject of authors who have had an impact on my life, I would be remiss if I did not mention Kahlil Gibran, author of *The Prophet*. This masterpiece was copyrighted by the author in 1923. As did Allen, Gibran wrote extensively. On my bookshelves one would find a minimum of eight of Gibran's books. It is *The Prophet* that has received the most acclaim. It can provide anyone with a map for improving one's life. The mystical artwork that accompanies each chapter suggests deep anguish—a searching for understanding perhaps? The later is my interpretation and does not do justice to Gibran's awesome talent. A friend and I tried years ago to obtain a copy of the artwork and were not successful. Gibran was born in Lebanon on January 6, 1883, and died in New York on April 10, 1931.

When asked to name my favorite authors, besides the two mentioned above, I am at a loss because I have so many that citing one would be a disservice to the others. Likewise, if asked the kind of books I like, I would have to say no special topic and fiction and nonfiction.

# 4

Except for one tree at the west side of our dwelling and a few trees beside the shack mentioned above, the area was barren, dirt packed, and bereft of grass, trees, or foliage. There were pebbles scattered about the area, but this did not deter the children from running barefoot in the summertime. Thus, shoes were kept in good shape for school and Sundays and from wearing out too quickly. There was enough open space to allow the children freedom to run, play, and cavort. There was much camaraderie among the children and the adults living in the camp. Generally, adults were available and looked out for the children. A special treat, to which the children looked forward in the summertime, was when Rocco would be coming daily with his ice-cream wagon that was pulled by a horse. As he rolled into the camp, the children would run to meet him and then waited impatiently until he parked in the middle of the camp. Children were ready for him, some clutching the few pennies they had managed to save or beg from their parents. Some children obtained their pennies by looking for glass bottles that could be returned to stores for cash. Other boys sold newspapers at the train stop and, on occasion, let the girls help, giving them a share of the profits. Rocco's cones sold for two cents for one dip, and for another penny, he would add a generous dip. By his overall behavior, Rocco showed his fondness for every child who approached him. I can say without doubt that the camp children loved Rocco and his horse.

It was particularly exciting when, at varying times, the stockyard owners brought cows, horses, pigs, and sheep to the pens located behind the camp houses. Observing the animals became a favorite pastime for the youth. Prior to the arrival of the animals, the owners had the corrals supplied with vast amounts of straw. Following that, the boys made a huge pile of straw. Then it was playtime for all. The older boys somehow obtained a very thick rope—similar to that used for towing vehicles—made a large thick knot at one end, and then secured the unknotted end to the upper rafter of the corral. A kid on the floor of the corral would swing the knotted end to one of the kids standing by the top rafters of the corral. The kid would grab it, sit on or grab the knot, swing high several times, and then fall onto the pile of straw. It was a thrilling experience. Initially, I was too small to be a participant, but after I could climb the rafters enclosing the pens, I was allowed to have this ride. It was gratifying to be included in this activity. When I think of these times, it is with fondness and a smile. It was great fun, and the best part was that there was no admission fee!

Playing marbles was a game enjoyed by the boys and male adults. Girls were not allowed to participate in this game. A huge circle was drawn and filled with multiple dozens of marbles. The players then took turns and tried to get as many marbles before an error, according to the group's rules, was made. Then the next in line tried his skill. The squabbling was loud and boisterous but not likely to end in a fight. Another sport some of the males, who had rifles, engaged in was shooting the rats that infested the garbage dump. Some boys were quite adept at this activity. There was only one riffle accident of which I have vague recollection. A neighbor's son, possibly ten years of age, came into our house and picked up a rifle that was left on the kitchen table by my oldest sister's husband. The boy did not know it was loaded. My sister Trini, our caretaker, was sitting at the kitchen table crocheting. The lad, rifle in hand, pointed it at my sister. The gun went off, and the bullet hit my sister, as I recall, near her left breast and traveled downward and through her side. She was taken to the hospital. She was very lucky that the bullet missed vital organs. She survived but bore the scars until her death many years later. The boy was very shaken and remorseful, and his parents were quite upset over the incident. I cannot remember whether punishment was meted out to the boy. He did remain close to our family and always a friend until his death. The females resorted to less boisterous games such as Kick the can, Red Rover, jump rope, and hide-and-seek. Whenever our cousins visited us, they were invited to join any game or activity in progress.

A positive side to being brought up in the camp was that it was a freeing and an exhilarating experience to run and play safely and without restrictions, except for those imposed by parents and watchful adults, which were few. Because the space within the units was too limited to engage in play of any kind, the weather permitting, residents, especially the youth, spent a considerable amount of time out of doors. Winters in the camp were harsh. Sometimes the snow was so high that it was difficult to open our back door, which was flush with the ground. Little by little we children were able to push it open so that we could crawl into our cave.

Survival Within Two Cultures

A few years ago, I had a desire to visit the campsite. The area had been razed, leaving a smooth tan dirt-packed floor. Physical evidence of the existence of the camp was obliterated. The camp houses, the city dump, the stockyard pens, the railroad structures, and machinery were gone. If life ever existed in the area, it is in the memory of its inhabitants of years ago, many of whom are no longer living. A railroad train to Chicago still passes through the now-desolated area and, to my knowledge, still provides riders transportation to the Big City. Today the presence of a few semis suggests that the area may be used as a storage station for them. There was no one around to question.

# 5

Having provided the reader with a glimpse of life in the camp, I now continue with more personal issues. My younger sister, age one, and I, age three, shared a godmother through baptism, who, although having two sons, fervently wished for a daughter. She was about ten years younger than our mother. She, her husband, and two sons lived in one of the camp units. She undertook the task of taking care of us not only to help our mother with her large family but also to ease her yearning for a daughter. I had long curly blondish hair, and I was told that she enjoyed washing, combing, and fixing it. As I grew up, several relatives informed me that to brighten my hair she added something, which may have been lemon juice, to the water when rinsing it. My blondish hair made me an oddity in the camp. Unfortunately I have no recollection of this caring person and the care she gave us but know that she had an influence on how my life developed. She died in 1931 a year before our mother.

A major tragedy hit the Luis Lopez family, when, on November 20, 1932, our mother died at home after giving birth to a stillborn female. She was buried on November 22, my oldest sister Cecelia's birthday. I was four years old and have little recollection of what was happening. However, many years later, in the course of my therapy and hypnosis, I believe I was a witness to some of the activity before her death and surrounding her death. Giving credence to this possibility is the experience I had when in deep therapy, which centered on her death; deep reds and blacks I *visualized* brought me out of my trance in tears. Upon being questioned and learning the reason for my tears, in my therapist's mind and mine, this may give credence to the possibility that I was a witness to her dying. I vaguely recall the coffin being in one of the small rooms. A cousin and dear friend, Lupe, soon to be five years old at the time, recalls seeing my married sister looking for a suitable dress for our mother's viewing. She recalls seeing her aunt, my mother, in bed and then the undertakers removing her from the bed, placing her in a large basket, and taking it to the vehicle that was to transport her to the funeral home.

My mother was waked at home. I have no recollection of the wake but can imagine that I was bewildered by the activity and wandered around aimlessly and mechanically. I have a sense that I may have been curious and tried to peer over the casket to see its contents. I surmise that it was not easy to accommodate, in the tiny quarters, the many relatives and friends who came to pay their respects. I have no knowledge that anyone gave notice or paid attention to the nicely dressed infant that lay next to her mother's face. Through the years, I cannot recall that anyone in the family or relatives ever mentioned the baby, at least not within my hearing.

The only tangible remembrance of our mother's death is a picture taken outside of St. Benedict's Catholic Church steps. The casket was slanted on the front steps before the entrance to the church. To this day, I can vividly picture the two green doors at the entrance to the church. These green doors surfaced occasionally in my mind and sometimes in my dreams. How could I forget doors that I encountered whenever I entered St. Benedict's Church? Family, relatives, and friends surround the coffin. Somber, grieving faces are caught in the studio photograph. My two-year-old sister was held by our father. I stood beside him at the head of the coffin. My six-year-old sister stood at the side of the coffin, looking away from it. My older siblings, sisters, and two brothers surrounded the coffin. What still stands out in my mind is the sadness I often saw on my father's face then and after her death. I recall clearly seeing my two older sisters, Joan and Trini, sitting on the patio bench, huddled together in their winter coats, finding comfort in each other's closeness. To this day, I can close my eyes and envision a picture of my two sisters as they tried to deal with their sorrow as well as the sorrow on my father's face. Neither he nor did anyone else speak to the three youngest daughters about their mother or her death. Except for Joe and Wally's presence by the coffin, I have no remembrance of their presence after the funeral. I have a sense that they made themselves scarce so no one could witness their sorrow. By the age of four, I had lost two mother figures and a younger sister, who was never mentioned as having existed.

Aside from envisioning that I saw my parents working together canning tomatoes, I have virtually no memory of how they behaved toward each other. My uncle Manuel and uncle Benito and their wives addressed each other by the formal term of *usted* and not the familiar term of *tu*, both meaning "you." I surmise that my parents, too, addressed each other in this fashion. Besides the funeral picture, I have only one tangible item. It is a studio photograph of my parents and me taken about two years prior to her death. It is a photo I treasure. It has always impressed me that given my father's humble beginnings in the United States, it was important for him to have this and other studio photographs taken of his children at important events in their lives.

# 6

Being left with five daughters and a son, Joe, was not an easy undertaking. Cecilia and Walter, oldest sister and brother, were self-supporting. Our father tried to be mother and father to his large family. He assumed some of the cooking tasks and became adept at making flour tortillas. He and our two oldest sisters, Joan and Trini, shared the task of preparing our standard fare of tortillas, rice, beans, and, occasionally, chicken or beef soup on Sunday. I feel the need at this point, and perhaps it is fitting, to record a poem I wrote in the 1960s. I was then the mother of five children. At the time, I was involved in therapy to help me deal with other traumatic experiences, which are discussed in this paper. For ten years and then intermittently, for a total of about twenty years, therapy kept me in touch with reality. I was fortunate to have professional friends and acquaintances I trusted, who saw me through the difficult sessions. On August 28, 1968, this is the poem that was an outcome of dealing with some issues concerning our mother's death and aftermath.

## Death's Revenge

An overwhelming sadness fills this heart,
Tearing the mind and soul apart,
Feeling the helplessness of humanity,
Stripping man of his dignity.

Will the restlessness that prevails cease
Leaving in its stead a quiet peace?

It is a foolish stubborn pride
And anger at a Christ that died,
That forms the wall of resistance
That defies all assistance.

Underneath is but a small child
That leaves the adult wild,
A child that wants what cannot be
To tell her dead mother
I love you more than any other.
I'm sorry if I was ever angry at you,
For feeling you were not my mother true.

Mother, mother, why did you die
Before I could run to your knee and cry?

I'm sorry, mother dear
For any childish, hateful sneer
For any unkind thought,
For any sorrow to you I brought.

> You died and left me,
> And guilt never let me be free
> To enjoy the simple pleasures of man,
> Without paying for them over and over above demand.

The death of my mother was an event not understood by this four-year-old. Where I was once a normal, healthy child, I lost weight, had stomach problems, and looked anorexic. My father would provide chocolate and white milk to help me gain weight. It did not help. My stomach problems were alleviated by boiling an herb, *yerba buena* (good herb), which I drank daily until I no longer complained of stomach aches. The drink tasted bitter. I cannot recall when I began to pass out. I fainted at home, and it would occasionally happen in church during mass. Of course, people were quick to come to my aid. I have no idea when I stopped this behavior. Today, I realize this may have been a way for me to get attention and have someone notice this "troubled" child.

Most embarrassing was that I became a bed wetter, and in disgust, my sisters pushed me off the bed. In tears, I went to my father. He did not turn me away but tried to ease my discomfort. At times, I had difficulty controlling my urine. I was six years old, very timid in class, and possibly afraid to ask for a bathroom privilege. I had one accident in the first grade. I was mortified and embarrassed. I do not recall that the nun made me feel ashamed when she became aware of my discomfort and the reason for it. I feel compelled to say that this nun was one who always showed kindness toward me and to my siblings before me. She asked a classmate to walk me home. I was chagrined to have my classmates witness this unseemly behavior. I did not want anyone to see where I lived, to see the hovel that was my home. As my classmate and I walked along the railroad tracks and neared the camp, my anxiety level rose, and I could not allow her to walk me further. We stopped at the road that led to the camp (123rd Street). I told her that I could go the rest of the way without help. As I think back, this was the first time that I felt the pain of who I was and where I lived.

I cannot recall that our father ever made us feel that we were a burden to him. Yes, he was impatient with some of his duties. For example, when he took us for shoes, we were expected to buy the first pair tried on. As a result, later we had to bear blisters and sometimes corns on our toes. He was a strict disciplinarian and demanded proper behavior and correct usage of our limited Spanish language. English was his children's primary language. If our mother had lived, it is likely we would have had more exposure to the Spanish language. His voice was firm and sometimes harsh, depending on the importance of the issue. Our father was impatient, and whatever he asked of us had to be completed quickly. He did not have to tell us twice what he expected. However, he could be sympathetic. I do not recall at what age, but sometime after my mother's death, I began to have severe leg pains around the knee area, generally on the right leg. Sometimes during the night the pain was so intense that my crying awakened our father. He would come to my aid and, with liniment, rub my legs until the pain subsided. As I matured, I learned that the pain could be numbed if I bent my legs and sat on them. I no longer interrupted my father's sleep. This practice continued when I felt the pain during school hours and when I was employed at a job that required sitting. These pains were referred to as growing pains; however, they continued until I was in my twenties.

# 7

I learned to do things quickly so that my father would not be displeased with me. However, I cannot recall that he ever resorted to physical punishment. The tone of his voice was enough to keep us in line. His daughters were not allowed to leave the house with arms bared. Once, in my late teens, he made me go back into the house to dress in something that covered my arms. Never did I have to be reminded of his dislike to see us with bare arms. However, sometimes I wore a sweater or a short jacket without buttons over my sleeveless garment. As soon I was out of his sight, I took it off! Dating was out of the question. On occasion after we left the house, he would follow us, keeping his distance, to assure himself that we were not meeting a male.

At about age eleven, my confirmation godmother, Evelyn, took an active interest in me. She was married to one of my uncle Benito's sons, Lino, the cousin who had provided schooling and books for the camp. The family resided in East Chicago, Indiana, and subsequently moved to a small farm in Dyer, Indiana. For several years, during the summer months, I spent a few weeks with them. I helped my godmother with simple chores and played with their two young children, Henry and Rita. During these visits, my godmother gave me the mothering I lacked. Concerned about my weight, she provided nourishing food. A glass of milk with bananas became a daily breakfast food. Without question, the food, and undoubtedly the care she gave me, resulted in my gain in weight. These summer visits away from home ceased when the family moved to Blue Island; however, I was able to visit her often. And she continued to be a positive force in my life. In spite of the family's relocation to Texas, to Colorado, to California, and, finally, returning to Colorado, I visited them whenever possible.

Where schooling was involved, our father was particular. Whereas all the children in the camp were enrolled in the public school nearby, he enrolled us in the Catholic school about a mile away. Because students were required to wear uniforms, it made the task of clothing his children easier. I can recall with fondness that every Sunday morning he reached under his mattress, where he kept money. He withdrew the correct number of dimes to give to each of his children for the collection basket. Because four older children were already in school, and proficient in English, except for our father, it was the dominant language used in our home. He addressed us in Spanish. We responded in our limited Spanish and mixed it with English, now referred to as Spanglish. My father, at some point, traveled to Chicago for English lessons.

Unbeknownst to his children, my father had located a house less than a mile from the Catholic school, and he rented it. As children, we were never told of changes that would be occurring in our lives. After living in the house for about a year, the house was sold. It was back to the camp for the Lopez family! Sometime later, our father learned that the house was on the market again, and he bought it. By that time, he had remarried. It was with pleasure that we renounced the camp.

Going back in time, about two years after our mother's death, our sixteen-year-old caretaker sister, Joan, eloped through the night with a man years older than she. Since all five sisters slept in one room, in one bed, it was remarkable that she left the room noiselessly and left the house without disturbing anyone. Our father and his four remaining daughters were devastated. It was just one more unexpected, traumatic incident that we endured. Since my mother's death, it was the first time I noted, on my father's face, the pain this daughter had caused him. Eventually, I surmise that he learned that she had eloped with the son of a family friend. Our father never mentioned her or spoke to his children about her. Then, our sister Trini became our caretaker.

# 8

Throughout my grade school years, I was the only Mexican female student. At times, two Hispanic males were in some of my classes. My recollection is vivid when I think back to those years. I was shy, timid, and somewhat withdrawn. I cannot recall that any classmate made overtures to engage me in conversation. Occasionally, as I stood on the sidelines watching, I was invited to participate in games during recess. I was not a behavior problem, caught on quickly, and did well in lessons assigned. Some of the nuns were kind to me and used me to help slower students with diagramming sentences, English, and math. Other nuns seemed to be ill at ease with me and tended to put me at the end of a line. In the seventh grade, in church, the nun put me in the middle of the pew to separate the boys and the girls. In the classroom, she seated me between the two boys who were the most troublesome to her. I can only assume today that she believed they would not bother with me, and they didn't!

I could not help but note the difference in the overall treatment I received during my grade school years. Initially, I was the only one in my classes who had no mother, and I presumed this was the reason for how I was treated. It was not until seventh grade that I realized that being motherless had nothing to do with the differential treatment I discerned throughout my early years. In essence, I was a Mexican and of darker complexion. Because outwardly my overall behavior appeared to remain the same, I cannot recall that this realization changed the way I felt about myself. I had no knowledge of discrimination or racism and could not associate them with the treatment I received. Neither our family nor the camp residents ever brought up or discussed these issues.

In retrospect, I did begin to note that children of large families, not Mexican, of light complexion, too, were treated differentially. At times, after school, a few students resorted to name-calling or threw rocks at us. Nonetheless, school became an escape for me—an escape from the camp. As I became proficient in reading, in addition to my schoolbooks, I read and reread my favorite books from cousin Lino's camp library. Among my favorites were *Understood Betsy* (I was unable to locate the author's name), Jean Webster's *Daddy Long Legs* and *Dear Enemy* (Jean Webster was the grandniece of Mark Twain, and her heroine was an orphan), George Horace Lorimer's *Letters from a Self-Made Merchant to His Son*, Margaret Thompson's *Woman of Property,* and Nathaniel Hawthorne's *Scarlet Letter—*which I read at an older age. When I discovered the public library, I became a frequent visitor to it, and my reading interests expanded. I was becoming an avid reader.

In high school as in grade school, I was a loner, shy, and made little effort to court the friendship of any students. Most of the students behaved toward me as they had in grade school—left me alone. This time, I was keenly aware that my Mexican heritage put me at a disadvantage when it came to making friends. However, I honestly admit that I did not put any effort into becoming friends with anyone. This attitude stemmed from my fear of being rejected. The unfriendly behavior I detected toward Mexicans and toward me when in stores or in restaurants reinforced my reluctance to initiate any interaction with the Anglo students. I did enroll in the Spanish class and then joined the Spanish club, in which I took an active part. I was of help when it came to selecting Mexican restaurants in the Chicago area. In high school I noted that some teachers reacted similarly to me as did some of the nuns in grade school. Teachers had their pets, and I was not one of them. Intuitively, I could not help to note the indifference of some teachers toward me.

I can think of no other reason than dislike for the behavior of my geometry teacher toward me. It appeared to me that she deliberately embarrassed me in front of the class. I had hoped to major in math, but because she taught all higher-level classes, I let this desire die. However, I did not let her destroy my will to continue to do well in her class and, at the end, earned a final B+ grade. Her treatment affected me deeply as I pursued higher education. I recall, when in graduate school, I turned in a blank stat test paper. On the way home, as I drove on the expressway, with tears streaming down my face, her image appeared before me. My thoughts were directed to the stat test. I recalled that as I glanced over the stat test material, I froze, my mind went blank, and I was unable to work on any of the problems. It was fortunate that my English, typing, and steno teachers always gave me positive feedback, making my high school experience bearable.

My thirst for books continued throughout high school. By the time I was a sophomore, I had completed all the required reading for my English classes through the senior year. In addition, because I had earned above-average grades in English, I was excused from senior English. During the freshman through the sophomore years, there were two other Hispanic females enrolled. One of them dropped out of school at the end of the sophomore term. To the best of my recollection, there were about three males, who ignored me totally. I was a good student, most of the time receiving the grades I deserved, and was never a behavior problem.

After school hours, Saturdays, and summer vacation, during my freshman and sophomore years, I had jobs taking care of children. When I was sixteen, I worked in a cookie factory located near my home until graduation. I opened up a savings and checking account at the local bank. I went to the dentist for the first time. Shortly thereafter, I bought a life insurance policy. In retrospect, I wonder if the book *Woman of Property* was the impetus behind my taking the aforementioned steps.

I had a strong desire to go to college after high school. However, I realized that this was not possible. And money was a huge obstacle. I knew of no Mexican who had finished high school and dared to venture into the college territory. Nonetheless, the dream and my hunger for knowledge persisted. After being graduated from high school, I attended Fenger night school in Chicago, where, because I owned a car (purchased when I worked for the insurance company), I hoped to enroll in an auto mechanics course. The registrar vehemently discouraged me from enrolling in that class. He had an instructor take me to view the class currently in session. On the way, the instructor emphasized that because it was a dirty class it was likely that parts of my body and clothes would be soiled. Furthermore, he felt that I might be uncomfortable because all the students were males. I cannot say that, when he opened the door and I saw the boys, I was uncomfortable. However, discouraged, I then enrolled in female-oriented classes—sewing and cooking. I had sufficient talent in these areas and learned little. I was beyond the beginner class. The swimming class was added. Because I had virtually no experience with swimming, it was useful.

Subsequently I enrolled in and completed a cosmetology course in Chicago. With this training, I was able to augment my salary. Relatives and friends became regular clients. Generally I serviced them in their homes. This training turned out to be valuable after marriage. It helped with finances in particular when there was a steel strike that depleted our family income. Eventually, it paid for college courses.

As I think back to my youth, adolescence, and adulthood, I believe I went through life mechanically. Events in my life were constantly changing without warning. Nevertheless, I did well throughout the twelve years of school. School and books continued to be my salvation and escape from the quick turn of events occurring in my home. Always, my major concern was that I never cause my father grief or embarrassment by inappropriate behavior. Perhaps I had been directed thusly because I had been a witness to all the pain he had suffered. As a student in a parochial school, I attended Mass daily, Saturdays, and Sundays even through the summer months. When in church, my focus was on the mural painted above the wall of the altar. It was a portrayal of Christ praying in the garden of Gethsemane. These may have been the reason for my drive to do everything quickly and perfectly. In essence, I had to be good.

# 9

Details as to who was responsible for the reconciliation between our father and our sister Joan, who had eloped shortly after our mother's death, and when it took place were not made known to his children. Apparently Joan was reinstated as a member of the family. My sisters and I were delighted that she was back in our lives and that she and her husband lived in Chicago. Occasionally, we visited her and enjoyed playing with our two nephews. Sometimes the two of us went together and at other times we went alone. We had no idea that her husband drank. Generally, when we visited, he was overly friendly and sometimes he offered us beer. My sister did nothing to stop him. We had no idea that she was a battered wife until a neighbor made allusions to it and informed us that on occasion the police had been called. The incident about which I am about to write is still painful.

To the best of my recollection, when I was between ten and eleven years old, I visited Joan without either of my other sisters. We had planned that I spend the night. My sister prepared supper and I helped set the table. As we ate dinner, her husband drank, and after supper he continued drinking. Though trying hard, I cannot recall when he gave me beer, but I believe it was before and after dinner. I had never had any kind of alcoholic drink, so if it had an effect on me, I truly cannot recall. My sister remained passive and did not stop him. And being brought up to obey and respect my elders, and my sister not stopping her husband, I took the drink offered. I recall that when I was a little child and before my mother died, I loved to prance around, dance, and was adroit at self-taught acrobatic postures. Whether or not I acted in this fashion, I do not remember. If I did, I do not doubt that he encouraged this behavior. In truth, I may have enjoyed the attention given.

Until bedtime, my nephews, then about two and three, played with their toys and games. After helping my sister get them ready for bed, the three of us went to sleep on the bed in the living room. I slept between the two boys and slept soundly. As far as I can determine, I awoke suddenly with the dreadful feeling that something was not right. It may have been after midnight. The light from a streetlamp came through the window facing me, and I noted that someone was bending over me. I was terrified that if that I made a sudden move, I would awaken my nephews. To this day, even after years of therapy, hypnosis, prayer, and meditation, I do not know how I managed to get out from under the form that loomed over me without waking my nephews. I did and ran into the bathroom, locked the door, and put a towel over the latch so that it could not be pried open.

I remained in the bathroom, wide-eyed, alert, and fearful that he could still get at me. I may have been dazed and not aware that I was not wearing underpants. I stayed thus until morning and heard my sister at the kitchen sink. I carefully opened the door and peered around the wall to look at her. Joan would not look at me, kept her eyes downcast, and continued with what she had been doing. From the kitchen, one could look directly into their bedroom and see their bed. I do not recall whether he made some noise or motioned for me to attract my attention. I found myself looking into the bedroom to see him in bed, motioning for me to come into the room. He held something I could not identify in one of his hands. My sister had not moved from the sink nor did she look up. Today I know that she was aware of what he had done and was doing. Like a sleepwalker, I found myself walking into the bedroom. He put a damp object in my hands, and in seconds, and in total shock, I realized they were my panties. Their dampness confused me. Had I wet my pants? At that point, I do not recall leaving the bedroom or what ensued later. I completely blocked out all that happened after he placed my wet panties in my hand and remembered nothing that followed.

To this day, questions plague me as to how I returned home. Did Joan take me home? Did she give me a pair of her panties to wear and so forth? Though I have no recollection, I believe she must have taken me home. What did she or I do after we arrived at my home? To preserve my sanity, I believe I blocked out the terrifying visit to my sister and all that followed. Shortly after the terrifying experience, I would wake up in the middle of the night and, in tears, beg my sisters "to turn on or keep the light on." Their response was, "Shut up and go to sleep." My father, too, woke up and demanded that I be quiet. After a few nights of waking up my family and tearfully begging them to turn the light on, my father and sisters lost patience. My father, in a commanding and angry voice, said in Spanish, "Ya basta" (That's enough!) and ordered me to be quiet and go back to sleep. Obediently, I did so, and the experience remained stored in my subconscious mind. Even if I had been able to recall the experience at the time, I doubt that, because of shame, I would have been able to talk about the trauma I had suffered.

# 10

It was not until seeking therapy in the mid-1960s and in my middle thirties that bits and pieces of this traumatic experience came to light. My brother-in-law's behavior was a heinous act against my person. Psychodrama is a clinical tool used in groups by some psychologists to reenact a scene concerning an event troubling a client. It was used with me to portray the behavior of the perpetrator while I slept. It was expected that I would strike out at the man portraying my brother-in-law, make some noise, or scream. It would have been the beginning of the healing process. I remained frozen and still in the clutches of the nightmare. In spite of the many years of therapy, and at times hypnosis, I continue to want to know what happened to the underwear I wore, what I wore home, and how I got home that day. Did anyone note a change in my behavior? As noted above, I did panic at night and begged for the light to be kept on. I was afraid of the dark. However, I was not able to tell my family why and they gave it no importance. I do believe that I had buried the abuse and what followed deep in my subconscious. I could not let anyone know what happened that night on my *last* visit to my sister's home. I have hoped that if I could be rid of this wish to know about those pieces that still remain locked in my unconscious mind, true healing would result. I would be at peace with the trauma I suffered!

Today, I realize that my brother-in-law's heinous behavior toward me arrested my normal development in critical areas. Through therapy and hypnosis, I also learned that the dampness in the panties was not mine and shudder when I think of the other possibility. Often, I would remark to my therapists that "south of the navel I do not exist." Blocking out aspects of the dreadful experience contributed significantly to my inability to grasp or reject reading material that had connotations of sex and dealt with relationships between male and female. It is my sincere belief that I let such matter go over my head. I know today that I unconsciously would not allow myself to let any reminder of the events of the past unfortunate experience interfere with my life, *but it did*! It was not until after the birth of my third child and reading a pamphlet by a medical doctor about female/male issues that I allowed my mind to accept matters of a sexual nature. My husband never had any idea that I, despite my extensive reading, was so unlearned about life.

I have questioned whether my sister was a willing participant in her husband's act or was she, too, a victim. I do not want to believe that any sister would willingly condone or support such an atrocity. By bits and pieces I learned that life with her husband was one of physical, emotional, and demeaning verbal abuse and terror. I did not return to her home. For the second time, I lost this sister. Many years later, she found the courage to leave her abusive marriage but was heartsick that she left her six children with this brute, who also abused them. In poor health, she left the United States and found refuge elsewhere. She lived in fear that he would become aware of her location and come after her. It was many years later, on the death of our father in 1971, that she found the courage to return for the funeral. I visited her in her new home in Mexico once or twice before she died. I desperately wanted answers to some of my questions. However, because she was not in good health, I did not wish to cause her pain, and I refrained from asking questions about her husband's abusive behavior toward me.

# 11

After the sixteen-year-old sister left, my fifteen-year-old sister, Trini, assumed the role of caretaker. She received special treatment from my father and my older brother Walter. My father took her to dances, which he, too, enjoyed. My father and my brother Walter saw to it that she had pretty clothes. They tried to make up for the responsibility thrust upon her. Everyday activities ran as smoothly as possible until my father remarried in 1940, more than seven years after my mother's death. I was eleven years old. Friends had arranged for him to marry one of their nieces living in Mexico. She was twenty years younger than our father. We had no clue that he was contemplating remarrying. We were unprepared and shocked to awaken one morning to find a strange woman in the kitchen. She was quiet, had little interaction with us, and did not engage us in conversation. She spoke no English and our Spanish was limited. No doubt it was as difficult for her as it was for us.

Trini felt usurped as head of the family, and the friction between the two was difficult for our father to tolerate. And her "fun times" and new clothing had ceased. Our father's solution was to separate the family into two distinct entities. There was an empty boxcar nearby, where he set up housekeeping for him and his wife. His four daughters stayed in the original housing. A year later, in March of 1941, our stepmother had a son. He was named Manuel, after our Kansas City uncle. For the record, about three years later, my stepmother gave birth to Tom and subsequently to Tony.

Pinpointing exact dates, long after the fact, has not been easy for me; however, a short time after our father separated his family, our caretaker sister, then about nineteen, eloped with the brother of our sister Joan's husband. The three younger sisters under her care and, no doubt, my father were totally ignorant of her intent to abandon the family. I have no memory of how we reacted to this sister's total disregard for the effect her bold behavior would have on us. My father never brought up the subject or spoke about her. I do not recall that my two remaining sisters and I ever discussed Trini's thoughtless behavior. Considering the many changes to which we were subjected, I wonder if we were just numb. Further, I am not aware that my father ever reconciled with this sister and her husband as he did with my sister Joan. My father suffered another devastating blow and we lost contact with Trini. He maintained his stoical approach to life. After this sister's disappearance, my father reunited his three remaining daughters and his new family. We lived in one camp unit. Nonetheless, communication between our stepmother and us was limited due to the language barrier. Our interaction was limited to basic living issues.

It was years before we knew where Trini and her husband were living. I suspect that my father did not make any effort to locate her. However, Blue Island is a small town, and happenings such as her elopement do not go undetected for long. Undoubtedly, gossip reached his ears quickly. He never mentioned her; we never brought up the subject. My contact with her, if any, was negligible. There was never any closeness between her and me. I was never comfortable with her husband, considering that he was a brother to the one who molested me. My visits to her were rare until her husband died. Then my visits to her were not markedly increased and were brief.

Recently, my sister Mary and I visited a friend, Rae, currently in an assisted-living establishment. She was our next-door neighbor when we lived in the camp. Of course, the subject of Trini's elopement came up, and she filled in the gap as to when she left with this man. She said, "I saw Trini leaving with her boyfriend in broad daylight while she was at the camp's community water pump." Mary's response was, "What nerve!"

# 12

Graduation from high school propelled me into the working world. With a positive attitude and top grades in shorthand and typing, I naively thought that it would be easy for me to find employment in the business world. This was not the case. I applied to companies in Chicago and to a large insurance company with a district office in Blue Island. I had no responses to my applications. I fought discouragement and continued my search for employment. Eventually, I was hired at Western Union in Chicago as a biller. The job entailed typing charges incurred by those using the telephone to send telegrams. Soon after, I joined their credit union and enrolled in their savings plan. I received recognition from my supervisor for my typing speed. Nine months later, a representative from the insurance company, to which I had applied earlier, called my home. He was inquiring as to whether I was still interested in a job. I quickly answered in the affirmative. I could not turn down the possibility of working less than a mile from home.

Subsequently, one of the district managers called and made an appointment to interview me in my home. Much later, it crossed my mind that the home interview was considered necessary because there was interest in an overall picture of the background of an applicant of Mexican ethnicity. To my knowledge, the company had no one working for it of this ilk. It is my contention that the district manager's report was favorable. I was hired and began work in April of 1948. Among the company's national policy were two issues related to female employees. In essence, marriage and pregnancy were causes for termination of services. The first of these conditions to be rescinded was marriage and, sometime later, pregnancy. I was married and retained the job. Two years later, I was pregnant, and because my pregnancy was uncomplicated and not very noticeable, I remained in this employment for about eight years, retiring on September 1, 1953, four days before the birth of my first baby.

It was with mixed feelings that I endured the first year with the company. I felt that I was always on trial. I had never been in close proximity to so many Anglos. The operation of the office was in the hands of a district manager. Insurance agents were divided into five separate staffs covering specific territories, and each staff was responsible to an assistant district manager. The office staff consisted of a supervisor, an assistant, and six clerks, who were assigned various duties. I never experienced working with and being in close daily contact with this caliber of people. A few of them in the clerical group were my peers. I was terrified of making a mistake. I was somewhat paranoid and felt that everything I did or said was being evaluated. Furthermore, I had never had experience addressing or responding to Anglo males in the manner required. Overall, the employees were very helpful and made me feel comfortable. A bonus was that every year the manager and agents treated the office staff to a dinner or a play in Chicago. This was a new experience for me, as I had never been to a restaurant or to the theatre other than an occasional lunch at a local eatery. At the bottom of my anxiety was that I would not be allowed into a restaurant and I would be an embarrassment to my coworkers. In the company of my coworkers, I was never denied admittance.

The overall treatment I received by the entire personnel was positive. By their treatment, I was aware that the caliber of my work was above reproach. The personnel as a whole made me feel that I was a valued employee. I formed a close relationship with the senior clerk, Gayle, who became assistant office manager and subsequently office manager. I was treated as a member of her family, and often I was a guest in her home. We continued to visit each other before and after our marriages. These were some of the happiest times I had, and the first time in the company of Anglos. I felt that I was no longer an outcast.

# 13

While I worked at this insurance office, there were two harrowing experiences that occurred within one year. The management paid the insurance agents with cash. Payday took place on Fridays. Two females from the office pool made a trip to the bank, located about one block from the office, for the payroll. When they returned with it, they proceeded toward the building that housed the insurance office located on the second floor. One week, possibly between 1950 and 1951, as the two clerks returned to the office with the payroll, they were accosted by a man who tried to wrest the money bag from them. The two clerks held onto the bag, ran, and tried to reach the tobacco company's entrance on the first floor. Their door was open. The man, persistent in getting the bag, shoved the clerks; and just before the clerks reached the door of the tobacco company, the man managed to grab the bag and ran off. The footprints of the clerks, as they were shoved against the windows, were clearly visible. Henceforth, to avert this unfortunate incident from recurring, a male agent accompanied one of the female clerks to the bank.

A year later, to the date of the aforementioned robbery, an agent and I were the carriers of the payroll. As we approached the office,

I glanced to my left; and in my peripheral vision, I saw the agent handing over the bag. I reached for the bag, saying, "What are you doing, X?" and I tried to grab the bag. I glanced up and beheld a man, wearing a nylon stocking over his face, pointing a gun at us. It goes without saying that I let the bag go, and the thief got away a second time. Some of the employees of the tobacco company who became aware that something was happening outside their door came out, but it was too late. However, resistance may have caused serious harm to either one of us or to whoever came out to help. The agent and I were quite shaken as we made our way up the stairs to the office. Manager, district managers, agents, and the office staff were stunned that this robbery of the company payroll recurred exactly one year to the date of the first incident. It called for a change in the payroll procedure—agents received their salary by check.

After two years with the insurance company, in 1950, I bought my first car—an Olds hydrometric. It was not on credit. It was a cash purchase. What an accomplishment! I did not know how to drive! My youngest brother, Joe, gave me the first lessons; and soon, he drove me to the Outer Lake Shore Drive in Chicago, parked, and told me to drive. I thought he was being cruel, but I followed orders. It was like throwing a person, who does not know to swim, in the lake to learn the activity. Fortunately, the drive was not as busy then as it is today. Shortly thereafter, I met the young man whom I married about two and one half years later. While dating, he took up the task of improving my driving skills. He was patient and not critical of my lack of progress. An added bonus to having purchased a car was that now there were two employees working for the insurance company who had cars. The entire clerical staff was accommodated when staff outings occurred.

# 14

Gayle's marriage a few years after mine did not dampen our close relationship. We held parties for friends in our respective homes. Also, I was a hairdresser for her and the females in her family. When her father became seriously ill, I paid a visit to his home to see him. He had been given a few months to live. He died within the week of my visit. Later, it touched me deeply when his wife, Elsie, wrote to me, thanking me for the visit. She added that her husband had said, "Minnie came to say good-bye to me." I felt as if I had lost a surrogate parent.

Years later, at the time Gayle had planned on retiring, she was diagnosed with terminal cancer. I had introduced her family to enchiladas, and because her family liked them so much, I taught her how to make them. She caught on quickly, and soon her entire family was enjoying enchiladas on special occasions. When I was informed that her time was limited, I wanted to do something special for the family. On December 8, 1993, I made a large tray of enchiladas for them. When I arrived at her home, I sensed that something was amiss. I rang the bell, and when the door opened, I knew by the look on her brother's face that my dear friend had died. The first, truest, and dearest friend I ever had was no more. Our friendship of more than forty-five years had ended. It was not an easy time for her husband, her family, her many friends, and me. She was one of the most caring persons I had known and treasured the friendship we shared, which included her entire family. She was loved by many. I cannot ignore citing that six months prior Gayle's death, her oldest brother had succumbed to cancer.

I remained a friend to her mother, Elsie, and when I was in Blue Island visiting my family, I visited her until her death. Her mother and I became very fond of each other, and she looked forward to my visits. I was one link to those in her family that had died. I had learned that she and my father shared the same birthday, which enhanced our relationship. Many years later, when she died, I lost another vital member of my surrogate family. To this day, each Christmas, I continue to receive a card from her youngest son, Rob, keeping me abreast of what is happening in his family.

# 15

Although I was out of high school and working, my father continued his practice of maintaining strict control over his daughters' social activities. Dances sponsored by clubs, weddings, and celebrations for any occasions were permitted as long we went in groups or were accompanied by our sisters. I was not allowed to date. I admit that I was not above finding a way to date someone if my attraction to him was more than just friendship. And that someone did appear. He was a handsome twenty-two-year-old marine, whose family lived next door to my oldest sister, Sissy. He and two other brothers lived with their father and stepmother. The stepmother had a spinster daughter, who was unattractive and was more than fifteen years older than her stepbrother, the marine. I frequented my sister's home in the hope that I would catch a glimpse of him. I believe that he, too, must have found me attractive because in a short time, he called me. Unbeknownst to my father, every day after work, this marine met me by the office entrance to walk me home, leaving me about one block from my home. On Saturdays, we went to the movie theatres in Chicago. We always attended the early showing to return home around 6:00 p.m. and hoped that my father would not get wise to the dating.

This marine, with whom I was smitten, was a perfect gentleman. He was caring, polite, and not happy with the fact that we could not date openly. He tolerated the restrictions I had and did not push the relationship further than kissing and holding. I, too, was not comfortable with dating behind my father's back, but I knew that I cared deeply for this man. I had no prior experience with dating. I was eighteen but very naïve and totally ignorant regarding the facts of life and sexuality. None of my siblings thought to enlighten me on the subjects. It is my suspicion that they, too, were naïve. Although I read extensively, it is my belief that because of my brother-in-law's molestation, unconsciously, my mind refused to accept information about sex and related issues. Hence, I was not suspicious of inappropriate behavior on the part of his stepsister. So sometimes when the marine phoned me and I heard the stepsister in the background, I thought nothing of it. It did sound as if she was deliberately messing around with him for my benefit. I heard noises and voices suggesting he was trying to get her out of his room.

On a subsequent date, he appeared ill at ease when he told me that she had gone into his room when he was not there. She had scratched my face on the eight-by-ten framed photograph I had given him. It was a studio photo I had taken upon high school graduation. I do not recall how I responded to this information but believe I just chalked it up to jealousy. I was not suspicious of improper behavior because of the age difference between the two. I do believe that he was not the instigator in the situation that developed, or maybe that is what I wanted to believe. The reality is that he had served during the war (II) and recently discharged. He falls for a girl, me, whom he recognizes as not being up on dating and on sexual issues.

At the time, I was working for the insurance company and was the district manager's secretary. One particular day he asked me to remain after hours to take dictation about a very confidential matter. The letter was to be typed immediately and mailed. As I was typing the letter, my sister Mary called. She asked if I was going to meet the marine and, if so, that I should not let him walk me home. She would not give me a reason why I should not see him. When I left the office, he was, as usual, at the entrance. Hand in hand, we started the walk toward my home. Although I was curious about my sister's phone call, I did not let on that my sister told me not to see him. When we parted company at the usual spot, he kissed me and then walked away. His behavior did not give me any indication that something was troubling him. As soon as I walked in the door, my sister handed me the local newspaper, pointing to the section listing marriage licenses. My marine and the stepsister had applied for a marriage license. I was stunned, not wanting to believe what I read. It was like a nightmare. I would not allow myself tears. I did not want my family, especially my father, to know the depth of my hurt. Like my father, I was stoic.

Again, my godmother, Evelyn, came forth to give me the support and caring I so desperately needed. Either she read the news in the paper or someone called her. She called me to offer the privacy of her home if he should call and want to see me. He did call, and I told him about my godmother's offer. I gave him her address, and we agreed to meet within the next hour. My godmother accorded us the privacy we needed. He was speechless and looked at me with heart-rending sadness. I held this marine, who had been through the war, as he sobbed throughout our meeting. He seemed lost and unable to talk about it or give me an explanation for his hopeless situation. I did not pursue the matter and believe I, too, was speechless. I do not recall how long I held him. It was extremely painful for both of us. I cannot recall what was said, if anything, upon parting. I do not remember ever shedding any tears and went to work the next day as if nothing unusual had happened in my life. I believe most had heard or read the news. The office seemed to be unusually quiet. I did not want anyone to witness my pain. Although the fact that the marine's stepsister was pregnant was common knowledge, no one in my family, relatives, friends, or coworkers mentioned it to me or asked questions. Their silence and kindness was the balm I needed. The woman was pregnant and a civil marriage was imminent. After the civil marriage, the marine left the area and moved to Chicago to live with one of his brothers and his wife.

For several months, with mixed feelings, I visited him in Chicago at his brother's home. I was not comfortable meeting in his brother's home. He was not comfortable coming to Blue Island. Soon I began to feel that I could not continue the relationship. The town in which we lived was small, and everybody knew everyone's business. If there had been gossip, I never heard it, and no one ever brought up the subject to me. I felt that everyone was talking about us behind my back, or they were trying to spare my feelings. As painful as it was, I made up my mind to break off the relationship. On the last visit, we met at a corner drugstore on a busy Chicago street. I had taken a radio, a watch, and a few other things he had given me with the intent of returning them to him. It pained me to have them in my possession as a constant reminder. He refused to accept them. I laid them on the sidewalk, walked away, and did not look back. It was a very difficult decision, but I knew that I was not mature enough to handle what could possibly happen if we continued to have a relationship. I would not be able to tolerate the gossip that was sure to follow and the birth of his child, who, undoubtedly, would continue to live in Blue Island. If my father was aware of my predicament, he never let on or approached me about it.

Henceforth, neither the marine nor I made the effort to contact each other. However, periodically, my sister Mary informed me that this marine made inquiries about me to mutual acquaintances. In the 1970s, I learned he underwent back surgery that resulted in paralysis. He was confined to a wheelchair and resided in a nursing home in Illinois. My response was that he did not deserve to end his life in this fashion. My sister continued to tell me that she heard from some of his friends that he wanted to see me. I responded it was not fair to my husband if I were to visit an old boyfriend. After hearing several times from friends about his request, my sister said that she would accompany me if I chose to see him. She believed that it was important for both of us and encouraged me to make the visit. I was uneasy about the visit because I did not want to be disloyal to my husband.

After giving it considerable thought, in the end, I picked up a carton of cigarettes; and my sister and I made the trip to the nursing home. It was painful for me to see this handsome marine in a wheelchair, the left side of his face drooping, distorting a once beautiful smile. Making conversation was not easy. My sister did most of the talking, and it revolved around impersonal questions and answers. The matter of his relationship with the stepsister and subsequent marriage to her was avoided. I chose not to bring up what had been a dreadful experience for both of us. After a while, he asked if we would like to see a picture of his daughter. We answered in the affirmative and followed him to his room. Her framed picture was on a small table beside his bed. We told him that his daughter was very pretty and that we were happy that he had someone dear to him in his life. He never mentioned her mother. My sister and I presumed that he was divorced.

We returned to the waiting room and prepared to leave. With a heavy heart and some anxiety, I leaned over, kissed him on the cheek, and then turned to walk toward the exit. My sister said good-bye and followed me to the door. I did not look back. It was an experience with mixed feelings and with some guilt, thinking that perhaps I had betrayed my husband. About three months later, my sister called the university where I was enrolled and left a message that the marine had died. Never have I regretted my visit. I appreciated the fact that my sister Mary did not let up on giving me information about the marine's desire to see me.

# 16

Chasing boys and being flirtatious were not behaviors in which I engaged. Nonetheless, I did enjoy talking and dancing with them. Because of my father's disapproval of dating, dating was limited and generally without my father's knowledge. After the aforementioned marine, I dated another marine briefly. He was serious about a commitment, which I feared, and terminated the relationship with him. Shortly thereafter, I met someone who, not knowing about my father's disapproval of dating, called for me at my home. No sneaking! Surprisingly, my father showed a liking for this bright red-haired, freckled young man named Rudy from Indiana. He invited him in, was cordial to him, never objected to his calling for me at home, and never voiced disapproval to me. It was not unusual for Rudy to find me with my nose in a book. He was patient and waited until I finished a sentence or paragraph. I learned later that Rudy liked to read, hence his tolerance to my interest in reading.

At the age of seventeen, Rudy, along with several close friends, enlisted in the United States Army on September 11, 1946. He received an honorable discharge on January 26, 1948, with the classification private first class. He was the recipient of the Army of Occupation Medal, Japan, and the World War II Victory Medal. We never spoke about his army experience. He bought a used car with which Rudy drove himself and his East Chicago, Indiana, friends to dances and parties. It was at a party in Blue Island, Illinois, my hometown, where I met him. His bright red hair was noticed by all who attended the party. In addition, the bright yellow sweater enhanced his red hair. He and I danced together the entire evening. He did not leave my side. The following week, there was another party. Rudy was mortified when he saw me walk past him and spoke to one of his friends. I must have been blind not to have noticed him. I was glad that my lack of recognition did not deter him from asking me to dance.

Rudy was handsome, loved to dance, and was sought after by many girls. He was not interested in them. I was impressed by this facet of his personality. After dating for about two years, I was taken by surprise when, on Christmas Eve, he surprised me with an engagement ring. I was stunned and speechless. I do not remember if or how I responded to Rudy. We had never talked about marriage, and in truth, I was somewhat fearful about it, given the examples I had with my older sisters' marriages. Afterward, Rudy took me home, kissed me, and left me at the door still in shock. My father was already in bed but not asleep, probably waiting for my return home. I went to him and showed him the engagement ring. He asked no questions but undoubtedly assumed that it was from Rudy. I presumed he showed his approval by saying that we should be married as soon as possible. It may not be believed by many that at age twenty-two I was clueless as to why my father responded as he did. Many years later I became aware of his reason—fear of pregnancy.

In the two years of dating, I learned that Rudy, except for an occasional beer, did not drink; smoking was negligible; and he was not a womanizer. He was taking classes in accounting at a local university. He enjoyed playing cards with his friends, who liked to play for money. Although Rudy was very lucky and often won, taking his friends' money was not to his liking. In my opinion, these were positive attributes. He was always ready to do something different. Once, although I had a round-trip ticket to Denver when I went to visit my godmother, he wanted to drive there and bring me back. He would not be dissuaded. So with my younger sister Marge and my sister-in-law, Angie, the three took off on a Friday night in my Olds and returned with me, in tow, on Sunday evening. What a trip! At that time, if Colorado had speed limits, they were lax. Except for his army experience and visiting relatives in Wisconsin, I believe it was the first trip for Rudy away from home.

# 17

Putting aside my fears and anxiety, I accepted Rudy's proposal and proceeded to prepare for the wedding. It was 1951 and we set April 21 as the date. The responsibility for bringing together all issues involved was in my hands. My sisters and friends were ready to help. Except for giving away the bride, my father took no active part. He made no offer to help me financially with the wedding. A neighbor, a professional seamstress, was employed to make both the bride's and the attendants' dresses. I was explicit in requesting that my veil be designed so that it did not go over my face. A bridal shower was given by my bridesmaids. Afterward, male wedding members and friends joined the party. It was to be a church wedding in the morning with a reception and dance taking place in the evening. The food was prepared by relatives and friends. My office coworkers graciously offered to serve the dinner. The guest list consisted of relatives and friends and included all employees with whom I worked.

To this day, I can recall vividly some aspects of the religious ceremony. My father and I were driven to the church by a relative. During the trip, my father and I were somber and did not converse.

By the look on his face, I surmised that he was concerned about the step I was taking. I was on the verge of tears. We descended from the car and walked into the church. As the organist played selected music, the bridesmaids began the walk toward the altar, where the groomsmen awaited their partners. At the back of the church, I took my father's arm as the wedding march began. By this time, I was having trouble holding back the tears that had been forming. With each step toward the altar, tears could not be contained. Many of the female attendants, relatives, and guests, too, noticing my tears, were tearful. I recall being annoyed when a female guest would reach out to put my veil over my face. I flipped it backward. I am clueless as to what I was thinking about that prompted tears. My feelings were mixed with anxiety, uncertainty as to what I was getting into, the state of my older sisters' marriages, leaving home, and so forth.

What my future husband may have been thinking as he stood by the altar awaiting his tearful bride was not known nor did I ask. My father turned to Rudy and presented me to him wordlessly. Arm in arm, we walked toward the priest, who awaited us. The tears were flowing as the priest repeated three times, bending lower each time, to hear my response as to whether I would take this man to be my lawful husband. After the third time, I said yes in a barely audible voice. When the time came to present a floral bouquet to the Blessed Virgin, the thought that ran through my mind was that I would do all within my power to make my marriage work. I think fondly of my husband as he told me later that if I had not wanted to get married then, he would have waited for me.

The festivities that evening were tearless and happy on my part, and all the guests appeared to be having a great time. Rudy was a fun-loving man and a gracious groom. The only incident that put a damper on the reception was that someone had stolen the cases of beer. The cases had been placed outside the banquet hall's service door to be within easy reach as needed. Fortunately there were kegs of beer on hand. As is customary, the bride and groom left early, leaving the guests to continue partying. We had decided to travel to the Ozarks for our honeymoon, and that we did.

# 18

The first hurdle Rudy and I had to face was finding a place to rent in Blue Island so that I would be close to work and Rudy's drive to Inland Steel would be less complicated. At Inland, he was employed as a hotbed operator. As pointed out earlier, I had experienced discrimination because of my ethnicity. However, because of the positive experiences I had with everyone at my place of employment, it did not occur to me that it would not extend to finding housing. I approached two possible vacancies in person and was refused tenancy. The thought occurred to me that perhaps it was due to my ethnicity. My coloring suggested to most that I am Mexican. My husband's red hair and freckled face belied the fact that he was of the same ilk. Afterward when I made phone calls to find housing and was refused, I asked whether the issue of being Mexican entered into the refusal. I assured the landlord/owner that I would not consider suing or making a big deal of it if that were the case but that I would sincerely appreciate it if they would be truthful. The answer was as I suspected. For more than two weeks, we stayed with my brother Walter in Chicago.

My father had an apartment in the second level of his home, which was occupied. With some concern about the current occupants, I asked my father if he would ask them to vacate the apartment so that we would have a place to live. My father was apologetic to the occupants as he asked them to vacate the apartment for the benefit of his children. The occupants, understanding the need for my father's request, agreed to vacate the apartment immediately. We had no furniture. Moving was easy.

Paying the required rent, Rudy and I made our first home in the upper level of the house which had been my home until my marriage. Rudy continued driving to his place of employment in East Chicago, and I had an easy walk to the office. This small apartment became a meeting place for Rudy's bachelor friends from East Chicago. On weekends they congregated at our apartment to play their favorite card game—poker. Sometimes, depending on their work schedule, they continued playing throughout the weekend. It was not unusual to find them awake and still playing on Monday morning as I left for work. And when I returned from work, I found, as usual, the sink full of dirty dishes. I busied myself to wash them.

Pregnancy followed about two years after marrying. I was in good health, and no unforeseen negative aspects due to pregnancy were anticipated. I continued working until four days before my delivery date. It was an unwritten decision that I would not continue working for the company after the birth of our baby. Furthermore, Rudy and I made the decision to make our home in Indiana. Thus, his commute to work would be less stressful. Reminding the district manager and office staff that my service with the company would end at the end of the week or four days before my delivery date was not easy undertaking. Throughout the last days, I had difficulty holding back tears. Whenever one of my office mates or an agent spoke to me, I answered tearfully. The seven and a half years of employment with the company had been an uplifting and rewarding experience. It was the end of a very significant period in my life.

# 19

Although I was aware that my mother died giving birth to a stillborn female, I do not recall being concerned with the prospect of pregnancy and the unknown. However, as the time drew near for my delivery, I could not dismiss a recurring thought that something could happen. I do know that I was deathly afraid of anesthesia and had made up my mind that I would not allow it to be used on me. I wanted to be awake and realized that behind my fear was what had happened to my mother. Despite excruciating pain, I rejected all efforts to put me under. I will never regret my determination to be awake. Fearfully, I tolerated the pain, and at the exact time of delivery, at the foot end of the delivery table, a beautiful lady surrounded by a dazzling blue-white light appeared. Was it my mother or the Blessed Virgin? Fear left me and I felt at peace. I did lose my fear of pregnancy. I vehemently refute the idea, as some propose, after hearing about my experience, that it was the anesthesia at work. I had not allowed it to be used. To have used it, I would not have visualized the beautiful lady, and it would have prevented me from the joy I felt when my baby, Damian, was placed on my stomach.

After bringing our son home from the hospital, he cried constantly, and writhed as if in pain, especially after finishing his bottle of formula. Rudy, relatives, and friends tried to allay my concern by telling me that it was probably colic or that I was a nervous new mother. His discomfort was eased after he regurgitated the entire contents of his bottle. He spewed its contents all over himself, the surrounding area, and me. Then he seemed to relax. In addition, I noted that he was losing weight. He weighed eight pounds, three ounces at birth. Whenever he was laid down, he cried as if he was hurting. He was only comfortable when he was in my arms. Often, when Rudy returned home from his midnight shift, it was not unusual for him to find our son in my arms, both of us asleep. Rudy was concerned too but tended to agree with others that I was just anxious and tried to assure me that it was nothing major. He was not always around when our son spewed the contents of his bottle. However, one evening when Rudy was present, he did witness the behavior that concerned me. After giving our son a bath, I laid him on his back wearing only a diaper and gave him a bottle. After he finished the bottle, we were both shocked to note that his stomach continued undulating, stopping as soon as his stomach emptied the bottle's contents. Rudy was convinced that I was not just a nervous mom.

To shorten this story, I immediately called the doctor and told him of our son's inability to retain nourishment. That day, he had evening hours and saw us immediately. He requested that I bring our son and a bottle. When the doctor saw what happened after taking his bottle and noting that he now weighed more than two pounds less than at birth, he hospitalized him. A few days later, at six weeks of age, he underwent surgery to correct stenosis (narrowing or constriction of a passage or duct). Without the surgery, our son would have starved to death. A few days after he was released from the hospital, as I was examining his incision, I noted that the scar was infected. Our doctor saw him immediately and the problem was corrected. Shortly thereafter, our son surpassed his birth weight and thrived. Because the apartment was small and crowded, Rudy and I decided it was time to seriously look for a house.

# 20

Neither Rudy nor I anticipated any repercussion from looking at homes in a new subdivision in Hammond, Indiana. We had a specific neighborhood in mind and drove around the surrounding areas. We decided to ask his brother John, who lived in a neighboring town, for his opinion on our selection. The following weekend, the two non-Hispanic-looking brothers, both with red hair, visited the site and home of our preference without me. Both brothers were in accord about the home in question. They approached the agent showing the home about their choice, the agreement to purchase was signed, and a deposit was rendered. The full down payment was to follow shortly.

A few days later, Rudy, baby, and I went to look at what was to be our home. We, including Rudy's brother, were unprepared for what transpired. A few days after our visit, I received a phone call from the agent, who had firmed the deal with Rudy and in his brother's presence. His call was made to inform us that the agreement to buy the home was revoked on the basis of a poor credit rating. I was dumbfounded, as Rudy and I had excellent credit profiles and had the required down payment. I did not buy the agent's report concerning a poor credit rating. Recalling that a woman who looked Mexican, me, was not present at the signing of the home purchase, I pressured the agent to be honest and tell me the truth about the denial of our petition. He seemed uneasy about my request, so I assured him that negative repercussions were not intended. With much apology, he said that when the neighbors saw me the week following the signing of the contract to buy, they registered a complaint with the builders and realty entities. The agent stated that there was no other option than to avoid problems by denying us the purchase of the home.

I was devastated. Rudy and his brother were at work. I knew that I had to tell somebody. My mind raced to the friends I had at the office, and there I sped with baby. The office staff was appalled. It was a Friday; the district manager and all the agents, who reported on Fridays, were in the office. The entire office was in disbelief that Rudy and I were subjected to such an undeserving travesty of justice. The outcry of the manager and agents suggested that they were ready to confront the realty officials, on our behalf, concerning the denial. I cannot recall how long I was at the office nor do I know what transpired after I left. I was numb.

When Rudy and his brother returned home from work, I told them about the telephone call I received from the realty agency and my visit to the insurance office. Naturally, they were angered and ready to take some action. However, a few days after my visit to the insurance office, I received a phone call from the agent who had called about revoking our home purchase agreement. He informed me that upon further consideration, his company would honor the purchase agreement. I do not know exactly what happened or who was responsible for the change in their policy. I strongly suspect that my former employer or agents exerted some pressure on the realty company. I do know that the entire office staff was aware of what had transpired and pleased about the reversal position taken of our purchase agreement. And I would be remiss if I did make known my gratitude for the support the entire staff rendered.

With trepidation on my part, we moved into this nice but seemingly biased neighborhood in September 1953. My qualms were somewhat pushed aside when I learned that the Purdue University Calumet Campus was less than one mile away and my dream of continuing my education was within reach. The neighborhood was serene and quiet. I did not get a sense that there was overt animosity directed toward us. Within the year, I applied for licensure as a beautician in the State of Indiana. The requirements were met and the license was issued. By word of mouth, some of our neighbors learned that I was a licensed beautician. Initially, the majority of my clients were children. Neighbors found it very convenient to find someone nearby to care for their children's hair. Soon, their mothers sought my services.

# 21

Shortly after moving to our new home, I was pregnant with our second child. I did not have the apprehension I had with my first child. I looked forward to having the same beautiful experience I had when our son was born. The delivery of our second child was without anesthesia and without problems. It was disappointing only because it was without the previous experience of the lady in white to which I had looked forward. Rudy and I were delighted with our daughter, Marcie. And I was not alone when hunger pangs woke her during the night. Our fourteen-month-old son, too, was awakened by her cries. Then together we held his baby sister's bottle as her hunger was abated. Marcia was beautiful; tending to her needs was not bothersome.

Within three years, Rudy and I were expecting our third baby. Our family doctor was on vacation when the baby was due. Another physician was available to fulfill his commitments. This did not upset me because the doctor taking over his duties was respected by the medical profession and the community. He was noted for the attentive care he gave to his hospitalized patients. And because my first two pregnancies and deliveries were without incidence, I expected an uncomplicated event. This was not the case. It was extremely traumatic for me, not because if its difficulty but because of the extraneous variables occurring simultaneously as my baby was on the verge of being born. At the time, the hospital did not provide for individual or private delivery rooms. In a cubicle, only a white curtain separated deliveries; it was not closed! In pain and without the anesthesia I rejected, I saw and heard, as did my attendants, the conversation and drama taking place in the next cubicle.

As I was on the verge of giving birth, my attendants were called to assist my neighbor's medical staff. Her attendants were in dire need of help with their patient. There was a flurry of activity in her cubicle. I was a witness to a woman who may have been dying in the process of delivering her child. I was abandoned, apparently without concern for the imminent birth of my baby. In spite of the excruciating pain I was in, I saw, with blurred vision, and heard the relentless activity in the next cubicle. At some point, someone noted the open curtain and closed it!

My neighbor was in a critical condition, and my attendants were needed to assist, but it did not help me with my fear. Recalling that my mother died in childbirth, the drama next to me was overwhelming; I lapsed into unconsciousness. I recall nothing of how my delivery proceeded. Was my doctor there at the time the baby was born? Was I alone? The only thing I recall is that after my daughter's birth, when she was placed on my stomach, my reaction was to stiffen. This was an unusual reaction for me because I recall the feeling of pleasure when my first two babies were placed on my stomach. As I felt her on me, I lapsed again into unconsciousness.

I recall waking up in bed in a strange room, somewhat in a fog, and puzzled as to how or when I got to this room. My roommate turned to me and asked how I was feeling. I do not remember what my response was. She did tell me that throughout the night, I was irrational and not making any sense. She told me that my attending doctor remained with me the entire night, holding my hand, talking to me, trying to reduce the aftermath of my traumatic experience. I remember none of this. It is a practice that after giving birth, the baby is brought to the mother to be fed and held. With my first two children, I did experience the afterbirth pain for about three days. With this baby, intense pain was felt for about eight days, something that had not been my earlier experiences. I did not know what happened to my delivery roommate nor did I ask any questions about her. I believe that I did not even want to think about her or what I had witnessed and experienced. Uncharitable? Perhaps. My attending physician lived up to his reputation and for that I am grateful. He did not return to see me before I was discharged. If my family doctor was informed about my traumatic experience, he never mentioned it when I brought Judy in for a checkup. Later I wished I had talked to him about it.

After five days in the hospital, my third baby, Judy, and I were home. I took pride in the decision I made with my first child that when my babies needed to be fed, they would not be put in their cribs and their bottle propped up with a pillow. They were held in Rudy's or my arms. Unless there was an emergency, this was a practice I kept with Judy. She was a good child and seldom was she difficult to handle. Her two older siblings kept her busy, which relieved me when household chores needed to be done. Although I now was the mother of three children, the notion of attending Purdue continued to plague me. When I spoke to Rudy about it, he said the children were too young and to wait a few years before giving college serious consideration. Three children, household chores, and a growing clientele for the neighborhood children's haircuts did keep me busy. Except for a family of three whose side door faced our side door, I had little time to establish a friendship with any of the other neighbors. This neighbor's eight-year-old son developed a strong and caring attachment to my three-year-old son and was his constant companion.

# 22

I was witness to only one negative incident in our new home. I was at the front door watching my two tots: a son, age three, and a daughter, age two. They were seated on the front sidewalk playing. Soon some older children came out and started calling them names. My children looked up. They were not familiar with the words and did not know their meaning. They continued playing. Before I could react, a neighbor two doors away and at his front door observed what was happening. In a stern loud voice, he reprimanded the name callers for their behavior toward children who were molesting no one. The children stopped, went indoors, and my children continued playing. In time, a friendship developed between the neighbors and the Rincon family. Within the year, the agent who sold us the house called on us and commented on how well we maintained and made improvements on our property. Fearing the label "dirty Mexicans" that I occasionally heard growing up, I was relentless in keeping my home and children neat and clean. In truth, except for the one incident, no one in the family was mistreated by the residents living in the subdivision.

Most of the residents in this section of Hammond were young couples with small children. One of the couples, with whom we met occasionally to play cards, was considering driving to the Florida Keys. The couple approached us about going with them to share the driving and costs. Our female friend's sister and her husband offered the use of their new car if their travel plans materialized. This incident revealed a part of Rudy of which I had not been aware. His family had never taken vacations. Except for the weekend trip to Colorado, it is likely that his travels were limited to towns and cities bordering East Chicago, Indiana, his hometown. He was excited about our friend's offer. Each couple had three children, raising the question of what to do with them. Our host couple had relatives who offered to take care of their children.

The plan that solved our problem was that Rudy's brother John and his wife, Shirley, who also had three children too, wanted to get away, if briefly, from the humdrum of life. The problems were solved by mutual agreement that they would take care of our children, and subsequently, we would take care of their children. The trip planned would be for a week. Although there was concern among us about how our children would react with the switch, it did not dampen our excitement about getting away from the daily grind. We relaxed, knowing that our children were in good hands and receiving loving care. Except for his army stint, this would be Rudy's first vacation trip, and he looked forward to it eagerly. Throughout the trip, the four travelers expressed their views about the sites to be visited and where to eat. Agreement was easily reached. It was a pleasant and stress-free trip, and the friendship between the couples grew. After we returned home and Rudy's brother and his wife were ready for their trip, we reciprocated. After our holiday, we resumed playing cards with our friends.

# 23

In 1958 I was pregnant with our fourth child. Rudy and I decided a larger home was warranted. In addition, Inland Steel was offering a great incentive to its employees who were in the market for a new home. Briefly, with the appropriate down payment and the ability to pay the home off in ten years, we were eligible for this unexpected blessing. Rudy met with the designated officials, and to our delight, they determined we would be able to meet the stringent conditions. With the help of Rudy's brother John, an ideal house was found in a new subdivision in Highland. Our intent to purchase the house was honored by the builder-contingent on the selling of our present home. Our house was up for sale, and within ten days we had a buyer who met our selling price and was ready to move in. The rest is history. In rapid succession, our house was vacated and ready for the new occupants. Within the week our belongings, including furniture, appliances, and children, were on their way to the new home. And, voilà, the mortgage was paid off in *ten years!*

Although Rudy and I recalled our initial experience with the purchase of the Hammond home, we were not anticipating that there would be animosity among the Highland residents toward

Mexicans moving into their area. Our neighbors were friendly and friendship was easily established. The comfortable feeling we were enjoying was destroyed shortly after moving in. One morning our next-door neighbor, whose side door faced the west side of our house, phoned to ask me whether I had been outdoors. When I replied in the negative, she suggested I come and look at the west side of the house. To my chagrin, on the entire west side of this new home, four-letter words were printed in large bold black letters with permanent markers. Heavy washing could not erase the words. The police were called and subsequently the insurance company. In brief, the entire siding of the west side of this new house had to be replaced. The culprit was never identified. It was considered an isolated incident. Our neighbors were supportive and appalled about the damage done to our home.

Within a short time Rudy and I developed a friendship with the majority of the residents, and to my knowledge our children were not the recipients of inappropriate responses from or actions by their peers. Three months later, our second son, Mark, was born. He was healthy and caring for him was not onerous. In addition, I had three helpers—his three siblings, who kept him entertained. Improvements to our home began immediately after moving in. The basement floor was tiled, and the walls were paneled. It was decided that I could set up a small beauty shop. Rudy installed the sink which had been in our previous house. A hydraulic chair and hair dryer were purchased. The neighbors quickly learned that I was a hairdresser. Initially, most of my clients were children.

As with our previous neighbors, mothers were happy to have someone nearby to cut or trim their children's hair. Soon my practice extended to their mothers and other women in the neighborhood.

Some clients from the old neighborhood continued to see me for their hairdressing needs. Although I was busy tending to the needs of four children, a husband, and hairdressing clients, I continued toying with the notion of college but realized that it was not feasible at the time.

# 24

Rudy thoroughly enjoyed traveling and spoke about wishing to travel to Europe, a country neither he nor I had visited. For a second time, the problem was finding someone to care for our four children. Once we found someone to care for them, we booked a two-week bus tour of six European countries. The tour began with a nonstop flight from Chicago's O'Hare International Airport to London, England. I was somewhat apprehensive about the latter because it would be my first time traveling by plane. The seven-hour flight over the Atlantic Ocean was overwhelming to me. Upon our arrival in London, a tour guide met us and escorted us to the bus that took us to our prearranged accommodations.

During this two-week vacation, we visited England (London), France (Paris), Germany, Holland, Switzerland (Alps), and Italy (Florence, Rome). It was an exhausting but exciting trip. My problem was getting Rudy to leave a site so that we would not be separated from the tour. He was enraptured with the walls and ceiling of the Sistine Chapel. This was the masterpiece of the renowned Michelangelo. Afraid to miss anything, he was adamant in examining the features of each person and objects depicted. He seemed to be totally oblivious to my anxiety about missing our tour bus and being stranded. The latter did not happen. Fortunately, we did keep up with the tour's agenda, returning to Chicago as planned.

At the end of two weeks, Rudy and I were ready to return home to our children, who were on our minds especially in the evening, and to our mundane commitments. Rudy returned to his job and I to tend to the children, home, and my hairdressing clients.

# 25

Within seven years I was again pregnant and, on April 24, 1961, gave birth to our fifth child, a girl whom we named Wendy. Our older children were delighted with the new addition to the family. I was not aware that there were problems with her delivery, and she manifested no physical or medical problems when Rudy and I brought her home. However, I did note that she had a small vertical slit on each side of her temples. One of the marks seemed to be deeper than the other and had a slight scab that was not immediately noticeable. I cannot avow how these slits were made. As with my other children, I had declined the use of an anesthetic. I surmise that the doctor may have been having difficulty with the delivery, an anesthetic was administered, and forceps were used. I know I was not conscious at the time I gave birth. About two weeks after bringing her home, she began to cry, as if in pain, whenever she was laid on her back. We recalled the problems we had with Damian, our firstborn, but ruled that out because she took her bottle without vomiting.

Then one day, as I washed the back of Wendy's head and neck, she cried out in pain. I had no idea as to what was making her cry. I picked her up. She stopped crying. One evening, Rudy was on the midnight shift and at home when I was giving her a bath. As I touched the base of her head, just above the nape, she began to cry loudly. Then I felt a series of nodules or bumps. Panicked, I yelled for Rudy, who, too, felt the bumps—bumps that covered the area from ear to ear. Without delay, I called our family doctor, and when he was informed about the bumps on our daughter's head, he saw us that same evening. Wendy had a staph infection.

Our physician, who delivered her, prescribed penicillin three times per week for about two weeks; and thereafter she was treated with an antibiotic to be taken daily for the next six months. I was her major caretaker and the only one in the family who could touch her and care for her. This was necessary to prevent the spread of the staph virus to other family members. Her sisters and brothers, between the ages of three and seven, could not understand why they could not play with or touch her. To keep them away from getting near her was not easy. I was frantic whenever I caught anyone near her crib, trying to reach her. It was a relief when she was completely free of the staph infection and that no one, especially me, in the family was afflicted by this highly infectious virus. The doctor informed us that the medication might affect Wendy's teeth. There was a possibility that her baby teeth would be discolored, and it may affect her permanent teeth as well.

We were clueless as to how she had contracted this virus. At the time, I had read a magazine article that cited that an infection of this kind was being reported by hospitals. I wrote to the hospital where our daughter was born and called to their attention the article that was mentioned in the magazine. I mentioned that unclean forceps may have been used in her delivery and may account for the small breaks at each temple, resulting in the bumps felt just above her nape area. I added that I suspected that she had contracted the virus through the forceps used in her delivery. Of course, the hospital denied the possibility that our daughter had been infected at their hospital and that this virus prevailed in their hospital. The hospital's position did not satisfy our conviction that she had been infected there. We did not pursue the matter further.

# 26

Five children, maintaining a household, and managing a hairdressing clientele kept me busy. As the children became of school age, I was involved in the PTA and Cub Scouts and Girl Scout programs. In addition, I found myself being unable to say no to anyone who needed assistance or volunteering—if no one else did—when an organization needed another hand. I handled all the sewing and mending needed, cooked nourishing meals, and baked for this family of seven. In addition, I was the official barber for Rudy and our two sons and hairdresser for our three daughters. The latter was an asset to our budget. Doctor's and dentist's appointments were never forgotten and the checkbook was always in balance. Some relatives and friends wondered how I kept going. I tended to respond that I had a lot of energy, did not tire easily, and required little sleep. Still, the proximity of Purdue to our home kept alive the flame of my desire of one day being a student there. When I spoke to Rudy about registering, he voiced no opposition. His concern was the care of the children.

As I think back, throughout my life I felt as if I was on autopilot. Like a robot, my motor kept going; and perhaps, I feared that if I stopped, something would happen. I never considered that my past, with all of its unfortunate events buried deep in the subconscious and had never had closure, developed a condition that could not be worked away. Although at times I felt overwhelmed by the pressures as cited above, I did little to change my behavior pattern. In the early 1960s I began to feel that something strange was happening to my body. Describing the feeling is not easy, but I felt that I was splitting, that I was becoming two persons. I can best describe it as being continuous and repetitive waves, beginning with my head, that I felt coursing through my body. It was a frightful experience. When it recurred, I would go to bed and rest until the feeling left me. I may have lain in bed for an hour. At first, I did not take what was happening seriously, because as soon as I rested, I was back to normal and returned to my usual pattern of avoidance by activity. This worked for a short period. However, I knew that if I did not take drastic steps soon to find out what was causing the splitting; my mental health was in jeopardy. I let no one know, especially my husband, how fearful I was.

# 27

Before I could actively search for a professional to help me understand why I was having the splitting behaviors, I learned that an agency, at which I did volunteer work, had a counseling program. Its mission was to help parents in how to handle their children's behavior in a more productive and effective manner. The program director, Ann, is a licensed professional. Her years of training and experience revolved around working with children and their parents. I participated in a few meetings and interacted with the members who brought up concerns about their children.

Ann was astute in picking up on the problem areas of the members of the parent group. I was no exception. She sensed, her word, that I was "hurting." In the group, she had learned that my mother had died when I was four years old. She intuited rightly that it was not easy for me to refrain from responding quickly when anyone, especially my husband, children, and clients, needed or asked for help. Often, I offered before being asked. I was hurt when she asked the question, "Are you trying to be everybody's mother?" I had no reply. Without probing further into my life, she suggested that I might benefit by joining an adult counseling group, which met weekly and was led by a licensed clinical psychologist. In my mind, this was an answer I sought to explore my anxiety about the recurring "splitting" behavior. Without giving thought as to whether Rudy would support my considering a program such as this or how my siblings would view my need for it, I enrolled in it in 1963. It was the beginning of a journey back through time, one week at a time.

The reason behind my not asking my husband's permission or letting him know that I would be participating in a group therapy program was because I sincerely believed that I might not get the support needed. How could I explain to him and to relatives who viewed me as strong and capable of handling any situation that I was weak and perhaps falling apart? Since I handled the bill paying in the family, I managed to keep my husband in the dark. To appease my conscience, I was paying for the fees from my earnings as a hairdresser and not depriving the family. Later, Rudy found a bill from the agency, was suspicious, and questioned it. I told him that I was concerned about my mental health because of the frightening bodily experiences, splitting, I was having. He was unable to understand why this would lead me to need counseling. He was quite upset and not truly accepting of my *need for help*. My children were aware that I had a weekly appointment requiring that I be away from the home for about one hour. They asked no questions. I assured Rudy that one hour weekly for therapy would not create major changes, and the family's needs would not suffer.

To avoid further questions about the bills, I asked the agency that no bills be sent to the house. I assured the bookkeeper that payment would be made as scheduled. The issue was not brought up again, but I know it continued to be troublesome for Rudy. He intuited that I was still attending the group sessions but did not mention it.

It is my suspicion that he felt betrayed by his wife, whom he believed to be devoid of any weaknesses, especially those of a psychological nature. He believed that he had married a woman whom he viewed as capable of taking care of her. It did not occur to him that in addition to "her," I was taking care of five children and a husband. It may also be that he may have felt that it reflected on him as a husband if it was known that his wife had a mental problem. When had we, before marriage, thought to discuss our lives as children, teenagers, and young adults during the courtship? Many of us go into marriage with undesirable baggage that we may not want to remember or may think it unnecessary to divulge to our future husband. To tell all might have been detrimental to the relationship. Furthermore, some of my experiences had been buried so deep that consciously I was not aware of their existence.

# 28

There were five women in the group therapy program, which included me. During the first two weeks, I listened attentively to their problems but would not admit that I had problems such as theirs. I was sympathetic to their hurts but was adamant in stating that I had no problems that bothered me. The psychologist was not kind when he came at me with, "Then what are you doing in the group?" The manner and tone he used jarred me, making me realize that I was cheating the group. In essence, I was listening to and observing their pain but setting myself apart, inwardly boastful that I was not like them. To date, had I not been capable of handling my own personal problems without anyone's assistance? At any rate, the psychologist's direct question hit me in the manner intended. It woke me up, and my therapy ensued, therapy that was to go on continually for more than ten years and thereafter, as I felt the need. The journaling of my life's experiences and meditation are practices that I continue to this day. I recorded many dreams, and in reviewing them I was able to relate them to events in my life. In later years, I was fortunate to know professionals in the field, and some with whom I had worked, who would graciously fit me into their schedule to help with a stumbling block I could not crush alone. Sometimes as I talked with them, a light would go on and, voilà, insight! At these instances, professionals commented that all I needed was someone to listen.

After the rude awakening by the psychologist, although subdued, I became a supportive and active member in the group. I listened to the participants' personal problems and offered appropriate comments. Often, I sensed myself feeling their pain and struggled to hold back tears—tears that throughout my life I stifled. Still it was months before I disclosed some of the serious issues that had propelled me to enroll in the program. It was then that I truly began to identify with them. Sometimes it was depressing and discouraging, and I wondered if we would ever rid ourselves of the hurts we bore. In my journal, I kept account of the issues I brought up in the group in an attempt to gain some insight into my problems. The journaling included current happenings. I resorted to writing poems. In 1967, I wrote the following on pain.

### ENOUGH
The mind recoils at the thought
Of the pain the past has wrought,
And so the will asks reprieve,
For a little time to rest and grieve,
Before another wound is opened raw,
Before its impact shakes us with awe;
And thus for all time bury,
The pain that had not lost its fury.

At times the issues that surfaced were so overwhelming that discussion in the group was too threatening for me and the psychologist graciously saw me individually. In the following years, when I reached a stumbling block, I sought the services of a hypnotist. At times, an outcome was that a hypnotic trance would bypass the issue for which I was seeking help and bring me to an earlier concern—another area that needed attention.

# 29

Shortly after beginning therapy Rudy noticed a change in me. Heretofore, I had been at his and our children's beck and call. Since we married, I seemed to anticipate his need and was quick to provide what was needed, often before he asked. My hairdressing clients, too, were seldom refused an appointment at their convenience. The outcome of therapy was that I was not as quick to respond as I was prior to therapy. However, I was not remiss in taking care of the needs and wants of my family. Because I worked at home, I was available. In making the changes necessary for my mental health, there was a change in Rudy's behavior toward me, and occasionally he became somewhat impatient. He was unsupportive when I was too tired to respond to a long-term client's wish to have her hair dressed at her home on a Sunday. He verbalized his displeasure, making me feel guilty for the stand I took. That I was too tired was not a reason to refuse service to a client who had been with me for several years. This client, too, although I was apologetic, was taken by surprise when I refused to honor her request and never made another appointment.

I was aware that a change in my behavior would ultimately cause a change in another's behavior. The lack of understanding on the part of those close to me, which included clients, hurt and bothered me. However, it was a price I was willing to pay for my sanity. The alternative was not an option because it might mean hospitalization, and in the process my family would suffer. And I would not be available even for myself. My extensive reading had included matters related to psychology.

There was an elderly client whom I serviced weekly. She lived on the same block but across the street from our house. The six children she raised are now adults. In a short time, I acquired another surrogate mother, and we conversed easily about everyday problems. An often discussed subject was my obsession of enrolling in a college program at nearby Purdue. I shared with her my plan to enroll in only one three-hour class for the first semester. It was a test to determine whether this would inconvenience the family. The class would be scheduled while our children were in school. My client encouraged me to pursue my dream. I brought up the problem of caring for three-year-old Wendy.

During her weekly appointments, my client had become quite fond of Wendy. Perhaps at a subconscious level I hoped that she would offer to take care of her. Since Rudy worked shift work, it would be only one week in three when Wendy needed care. This gracious lady offered to do so. Then my major worry was how to present to Rudy, on the heels of the change in me he had quickly noted, that I needed to take the awesome step to become a college student.

# 30

As with the therapy, I did not consider asking for Rudy's permission to enroll at Purdue. This was the second issue on which I took a stand. I told him that I had decided it was time to make the move. I assured him that I would not deprive him or the children of the care they needed. To his credit, I do not recall that he tried to dissuade me from fulfilling a dream. Early in our marriage, I had encouraged Rudy to continue with the college course in which he was enrolled when I met him. I let him know that I would support him wholeheartedly. He did not take me up on the offer. I do not think it was because he lacked the intelligence but because he lacked motivation. It is my belief that he lacked confidence in himself and possibly ambition. I can recall to this day that once, when we were discussing the issue of college with friends, one with a master's degree, I remarked that I would be supportive of Rudy if he wanted to continue his education. He countered with, "But you are not my family." I remember this incident vividly and the hurt that I felt that he did not consider me family. As for what my siblings and relatives thought, when they learned of my enrolling at Purdue, their comment was, "What about Rudy?" I countered that with, "What about Minnie?"

In retrospect, I realized that what Rudy wished desperately was the confidence he would have gained if his family had encouraged him to continue his education and be supportive of his effort to improve himself. I am also aware that many have struggled and succeeded without family encouragement. Rudy, however, needed his family to believe in him by talking to him, encouraging him, and expecting him to do well in school. In support of my contention about his lack of confidence in himself, I recall that on at least two occasions he made a remark, once to our insurance agent, that "Minnie could take better care of the children than I could." He said this quite easily, but in my opinion, it was a sad self-indictment. And it did not make me feel good about myself. As a matter of fact, it frightened me to have this onus placed on my shoulders. His belief that I was capable of dealing with whatever life dealt to me was frightening. However, perhaps because of my childhood need to be good so that I did not displease my father and now not to displease Rudy, I continued on the path established as a young child. Until the time I realized that I needed help in the form of therapeutic assistance, *our home*, generally, gave the semblance of a happy one.

As I thought about what I had written above, it occurred to me that perhaps in wanting to do everything for my husband before he asked and trying to please him, I had done him a disservice. And it struck a nerve as I thought about my relationship with my father, whom I never wanted to cause grief. I had to be good, do everything right, so that I would not be scolded or make him unhappy. The most hurtful and only word he used when his children behaved in a manner that displeased him was *desgraciada* in his sternest voice and with an angry facial expression. Because we, the children, were dominantly English speaking, we did not know what the word implied but knew that it was said to express his disgust with us for the behavior

## Survival Within Two Cultures

in question. In writing this paper, I looked up the definition of this word. Following are some of the English definitions given in a Spanish/English dictionary: miserable, ungrateful, out of favor. At these times, although I was ignorant of the word's meaning, I was crushed and asked myself how I could have acted in a way that would prompt a father to use this term, a father who had suffered so much with the loss of his wife and baby and was left to raise six children. In fairness to my father, it was not often that he scolded his children. I cannot remember that he ever used physical punishment. The closest he came to the latter was making us kneel on a sack of beans for misbehavior. This did not occur often, and as soon as he was gone, our older sister Trini let us get up!

It was important to bring up the foregoing issue concerning my need to do everything so that I would not displease the males important to me, e.g. father, husband. I now understand clearly that I may have been culpable in adding to Rudy's lack of confidence. Sometimes when I was asked how many children I had, I responded "six" and then quickly corrected myself. Interestingly, except when he was at work or at some function, Rudy was the disciplinarian and was looked to for permission to engage in an activity. When he corrected our children, he tended to take on a mad, harsh expression but never did he resort to use a word that connoted the one used by my father and never resorted to using everyday cuss words in our home. He thoroughly enjoyed movies, and often, he would take our children. At times, I accompanied them. Camping was another outing enjoyed by Rudy and our children, and often, their friends were invited. Having been born and raised in a camp like environment, this was not something I wanted to repeat. Growing up, I had had enough of going to an outdoor pump for water and to an outdoor latrine. If he was not working, Rudy seldom refused to take our children to special school events and to take them to or bring them back from visits to their friends. He was patient and a very good instructor when it came to teaching our children, their friends, and our next-door neighbor to drive a car. Also, he was an active participant in the PTA. Rudy declared Sundays to be poetry time. He asked each child to select a poem to memorize and then recite it to the family. Although our children sometimes dragged their feet, they acquiesced to their father's request because the sooner they did as requested, the sooner they were free to go outside.

So in taking two drastic steps, therapy and then college, without asking Rudy's permission, his concept of self may have suffered. It is my impression that the therapy issue was more threatening to him than college. Nonetheless, my determination to get a college degree overrode the disapproval I suspected but that Rudy did not voice. Therapy had brought changes in me and was the catalyst for taking the step to further my education. It would be understandable that he might feel threatened. I was aware that I might be taking a risk, i.e. failure or put my marriage in jeopardy. Later, I was grateful that when I had a class and he was home caring for our two youngest children, he did not show overt displeasure. It is imperative to note that I no longer had the splitting behavior reported above. I cannot pinpoint exactly when I was relieved of this malady and my sanity was restored. I have not missed the feeling that I was splitting and have no explanation for its disappearance. Therapy did provide me with the courage and support I needed to put limits on what I was able to do without undue stress on me.

# 31

It was 1964, and I was determined to enroll at Purdue for the fall term. Purdue's Calumet Campus, in Hammond, Indiana, was housed in one large, somewhat-square building. Two stories held the rooms in which most courses were conducted. The basement provided the space for a cafeteria and additional rooms for classes. The first hurdle was to approach the university to register. I was thirty-six years old, the mother of five, and had never been in a college or university building. I had no clue as to what I was getting into. It was with high anxiety, kept in check by sheer will, that I opened the doors. Finally, I had my foot in the door and the entrance to my dream. I proceeded to the registrar's office. I was determined to enroll and managed to control the nervousness I felt. I have tried to recall this experience but remember nothing of the procedure or what steps I had to take or took. It is my belief that the therapy I had and continued to have propelled me to enroll in and opt for a BS in psychology with a minor in sociology. It was gratifying to learn that because I had three years of Spanish in high school, which I had aced, I would be given credit for them provided that I pass a Spanish literature course. This blessing would yield nine free credit hours.

The two classes in which I was enrolled for the 1964–1965 first semester were Principles of Speech and English Comp 1. The speech class met at 9:00 a.m. In high school, I never had speech. I recall being very nervous whenever teachers required an oral presentation. I entered the speech classroom and beheld a room full of fresh young faces. No doubt I may have been apprehensive and scared to look at the students. Many looked to be about ten years older than two of my older children. The professor may have been ten to fifteen years older than I.

Beginning with this particular professor was a blessing. To my relief, the professor seemed to be aware of the unease and discomfiture of this neophyte, older college student. He was supportive not only in class but in his office when I needed help with an assignment. He addressed me in a manner that put me at ease but not patronizing and always encouraging. When I think of my first professor, who is now deceased, it is with fondness. My young classmates were always friendly, respectful, and did not make me feel out of place. The major problem for me was to prepare the first speech and then stand in front of the class to present it. I cannot recall how many speeches were assigned—my guess, perhaps three. I recall the feeling of apprehension as I stood before these young students and delivered my first speech. The fear lessened somewhat throughout the semester but was never totally overcome. Neither the professor nor the students gave me the feeling that I was out of place. I felt accepted, something I never felt throughout my twelve years of Catholic and public education. I was more at ease with English Composition 1, where I received the same treatment as in the speech class. A grade of B noted for both courses.

It is not my intention to bore the reader with classes taken and grades received. Suffice it to say that I received passing grades in all areas. I was chagrined with the D grade in algebra and Trig II but was somewhat encouraged with the C grade received in Finite Mathematics—the class taken during my senior year. I had not expected math to be a weakness. Except for a B+ grade in geometry in my sophomore year in high school, I had been an A student in math throughout grade school and high school. I made reference to my high school geometry teacher earlier in this paper and the effect she had on me respective to her abusive behavior toward me in front of my peers. Except for the D above and a few Cs, As and Bs prevail in my transcripts. Because all classes were scheduled during the day, I was home before my children returned from school and throughout the night. I was gratified, when I came home later than usual, to find that my daughters Judy and Marcie had started supper. My husband worked shift work, and for the midnight shift he was home and available to our children during the day if his help was needed. Although he did not encourage or discourage me verbally, I knew intuitively that he would not try to stop me from continuing in the course I had taken. For this I was grateful.

# 32

In 1967 I did not enroll in a class for the summer session. With one year of French to my credit, I felt I could make myself understood and surprised my husband with the idea of taking a trip to France. Rudy needed little encouragement and was ready for travel. We decided that as long as we would be in Europe, we should add Spain to our itinerary and make it a three-week vacation. Our main concern was our children. We managed to find care for them and our plans were underway. We booked a bus tour with a local travel agency. Our three-week trip would begin with a flight from Chicago's O'Hare International to Madrid. We planned to leave the tour group and rent a small car to use throughout our trip.

In Madrid, we were awed by the Prado Museum of Art. The building itself is outstanding. The art treasures in the museum represent donations by private individuals. To select one or a few artists on which to comment would do a disservice to the other artists whose paintings are displayed. Rudy and I were awed by all as we visited the rooms, which housed the artists' work. A visit to Toledo, the home of El Greco, was not to be missed. The work and piety of this gentleman were awesome and breathtaking. Rather than staying at impressive hotels, our choice was the locally owned *pensiones*, similar to our bed-and-breakfast establishments. They were less expensive and gave us the opportunity to mingle and exchange conversation with the inhabitants of the country. Rudy and I spoke Spanish, which pleased them because they were able to exchange conversation with us in their language.

Leaving Madrid, we traveled north and headed toward the Pyrenees Mountains. Rudy and I had never been to Spain. Except for the map we used on our travels and information we obtained from the Spanish people we encountered along the way, we knew nothing about this area or what accommodations were available. We did expect and hoped to find a pension to satisfy our need for food and rest before driving across the mountains. As I recall, we arrived at a picturesque town by the name of Huesca. At the time we traveled (1960s), it was a remote, sparsely populated small village at the foot of the Pyrenees. From it one could look up and gaze at the majesty of the mountains. There, we found the accommodations we sought—the Spanish version of a bed-and-breakfast facility.

The owners of the pension were delighted that we spoke their language and graciously took our reservation for food and lodging. As I recall, we were the only guests at the time. We enjoyed leisurely walking the main streets of the town. All inhabitants, whom we had the pleasure to meet, were friendly, hospitable, and delighted that we spoke Spanish, making communication easy for all. We had questions from each other. They wanted information about the United States, and we, about the area we were in. Few of the townspeople left the area and seemed fearful of traveling across the mountains. Hence, they had no knowledge of what one might find across the mountains. A local man told us that the residents of the town firmly believed that once one left and crossed the Pyrenees, the person was never heard of again. The impression given was that the one who dared to cross the mountains had perished. The owners of the pension did everything in their power to make us comfortable and prepared a delicious dinner and breakfast for us. Along the way to the mountains, the few people with whom we came into contact were friendly, accommodating, and happy to exchange conversation with us in their language. It is my impression that because of the barrenness and isolation of the area, it was not often that they had the opportunity to meet people, especially Americans.

Traveling through the Pyrenees was a spectacular experience. On the Spanish side, the terrain was barren, stark, and devoid of greenery. A lone guard stood at the top. Scanning the terrain, it was clear to us that at present, he was the only human in this vast area. He exchanged pleasantries with us easily and appeared happy that we were able to speak to him in Spanish. We made a comment that this high, one could feel close to God. His response in Spanish was, "Si, pero muy solitario" (yes, but lonely). Without a doubt, at least for this day, we broke the monotony and silence he faced daily.

Driving down the French side of the mountain, we were impressed by the lush green terrain, a marked contrast to the Spanish side. The beautiful blue-green lake at the bottom was breathtaking. We could not resist stopping to enjoy this area. We sat on the soft grass and relished the calmness, beauty, and peacefulness of the area. It would be a great place for a picnic. With reluctance, we left and continued on to our destination—Paris. We stopped to refuel often and looked forward to exchanging conversation with the inhabitants. Many spoke some English, and with my limited French, we managed to communicate. Wherever we stopped, the people were friendly and greeted us warmly. A tot of one of the gas-station attendants approached me easily and without a semblance of fear took my hand. We took a short walk while the car was being serviced.

In Paris, our major difficulty was finding a restaurant that provided meals with which we were familiar. Rudy was more cautious about food than I. We stopped to ask someone walking along the street for a recommendation. His comments were not very positive about French cuisine and suggested eating at, to my recollection, Colonel Sanders. In Paris our major visits included the Sacre Coeur Church, the Louvre, and walking the area of the Montmartre. The latter is noted for the presence of talented artists who display their artwork in the streets. Presumably the artists hope that passersby would be seduced into buying a piece of their impressive work. It was in the Louvre, as I recall at this late date, that we saw the painting of the *Mona Lisa*. It was enclosed in glass to protect it because of damage done to it earlier and to prevent further damage. These sites were extremely pleasurable and had been musts in our itinerary.

We traveled along the western borders of France and Spain and then turned east, continuing along the southern coast of Spain to the city of Malaga, noted for its wine, and the city of Torremolinos, an art colony. The awesome talent of the artists was evident in the paintings displayed. In one studio, a religious painting stirred me so deeply I had trouble moving away from it. I wished that I had the funds to purchase it. We considered crossing into Gibraltar but believed it to be unwise. The residents cautioned against it, citing the prevailing unrest between Gibraltar and Spain at this time. Spain was concerned with the safety of their citizens who worked there and had recalled them home. Torremolinos derived its name from the numerous towers (*torres*) built along the coast to protect Spain from dangerous unwanted visitors, such as pirates. It is likely pirates are no longer a serious concern.

As we walked along a main street in Torremolinos, Rudy and I talked about being homesick and missing our children. We continued our walk, and suddenly we heard someone playing and singing American songs. To our delight, we looked up and saw that the strains of music were coming from an Irish Pub. Without hesitation, we turned into its open door. We received a warm greeting by the establishment and its patrons, most of whom were Americans and also homesick. Of course, we joined in the singing. It was a delightful experience and a great way to end our trip. We spent the night in Torremolinos, and early the next morning we left for the Madrid airport. In about seven to eight hours, we were in Chicago. When we arrived home it is difficult to say who was the happiest—the parents or the children. It was clear that we missed each other immensely. However, Rudy and I never regretted that we made the trip. The European trip was motivation for me to continue with my studies. And I did!

On June 7, 1968, the Lopez families were saddened by the death of the youngest Lopez brother, Benito. It was the day after the death of Robert Kennedy. At will, I can still visualize my uncle's cheerful nature and smiling face and recall the warmth with which he treated us, his nieces.

# 33

One of the courses in business and industry not only gave me credit but also a pleasurable and novel experience with some of the students who were a few years older than my oldest children. The major requirement for the course was that students set up a business with the intent of making a profit. The professor divided the students into three or four equal groups. To the best of my recollection, the group to which I was assigned included five males. As a group, a decision had to be made as to what business could be set up, be completed within the semester, and assure us of a profit.

After brainstorming our options and being realistic about what we would be able to accomplish within the semester period, we were fortunate in having a member of the group who was proficient in art and adept in silk-screening. A plus, he had the equipment needed. Also, Purdue had changed its logo and we intended to profit by it. We were in agreement that our business would entail silk-screening bath and beach towels and blankets with the new Purdue emblem. With easy access to our major clientele—the students—we had customers at hand. In addition, we assumed that outsiders—e.g., alumni, parents, Purdue fans, and the general public, too—were potential customers for these products with the new Purdue logo. The next obstacle was where to set up our mini factory. The males in the group were single, possibly living at home or perhaps living on their own. Time was of the essence. To seek a parent to ask for the use of one's home for a project that would expose the occupants to strong fumes from the chemicals necessary would consume time we could not afford. I stepped in, assured that Rudy would not mind, and offered our basement. It was not surprising that all agreed to accept this offer, and our venture into the business world began.

We were kept busy, as demand for our products continued to the end of the term and beyond. We were profitable, and at the end, the earnings were divided among the workers. All of the members appeared for work as scheduled and pitched in to do the work required. Not one of us dragged his feet. I must mention that the members, without my knowledge, decided to award me a larger portion of the earnings because my home was put at their disposal. Their decision and generosity were unexpected and thoughtful. The cost, if there was any, to having the group set up our mini factory in our home was never an issue. I was blessed to have been a member of this group of young energetic men. At the time, I had never had the experience of being around silk-screening or been exposed to the chemicals used. To my knowledge, the fumes did not harm the employees nor did Rudy and our children exhibit health problems. My children were excited about what was going on in their basement. Often, from the top of the stairs, they peeked or came down the stairs to see the activity more closely. It was a pleasure and a rewarding experience to be considered and treated as an equal by these young men and never made to feel out of place. In so many ways, it was a rich learning experience for me.

On June 9, 1970, Purdue University Calumet Campus graduated me with a Bachelor of Science degree with the area of concentration, psychology. I don't recall that any member of my family was impressed by what I had accomplished. My father may have had conflicting feelings because in our ethnic group it was unheard of that women were encouraged to seek education beyond elementary school, if that. I never knew him to comment to anyone about my pursuit of higher education. He never gave any indication that he was proud of me. However, he never praised me when through grade and high schools A grades prevailed. It touched me deeply that my husband insisted that I have a studio portrait in honor of my accomplishment. He was well aware of my reluctance to have any pictures taken of me. He, however, was ready with a camera to take pictures of the family activities and of the trips taken. After realizing how much it meant to him, I traveled to Chicago to be photographed.

Therapy was something that I was not ready to abandon and continued it, knowing that Rudy was uncomfortable with it. I believe that around this time I shared some issues, one of which I believe affected him greatly. I asked him to join me in therapy and he agreed. I set up a date with the psychologist, who, the day before our meeting, called to cancel the appointment because of an unanticipated emergency. I set up another appointment, which Rudy refused to attend, saying that when he had been ready, it had been cancelled. I do not think I would be remiss in thinking that this was a cop-out on his part. Because of the nature of this serious issue, I believe the topic would be threatening to him. This was a period in my therapy where I needed Rudy's support and for him to understand that neither he nor I was responsible for the problems of my childhood. After divulging myself, there appeared to be a distance in our relationship. I do regret that we were never able to resolve the problems that no doubt had a negative impact on our marriage. Through the years, I learned that Rudy's home life was not without unfortunate incidences. He may have feared entering into therapy with me would bring out painful memories of his life that he would rather not reveal.

# 34

With encouragement from my mentor and advocate and his belief that I could handle graduate work, I enrolled in two advanced education courses for the summer session of 1970. Then in September, a Purdue colleague informed me the Hammond Department of Public Welfare was in dire need of a bilingual caseworker and encouraged me to apply. I did apply and was hired on October 1970. I was assigned the Cuban refugee caseload. A few years earlier, I read a book by Rene Dubois about Cuba's political climate, and now working directly with the Cuban refugees, it gave me firsthand information about the Cuban crisis and the plight of its citizens. It brought me in close contact with the food and medical shortages and the atrocities foisted upon many of its inhabitants. I was impressed by the courage they manifested in leaving their country and all their possessions to start anew in the United States. The financial and medical assistance provided to them by the United States helped to ease the transition—at least financially. As a whole, the Cuban refugees on my caseload treated me with warmth and friendship. It was not long before I learned to drink coffee as made by them. This was a feat because I was not a habitual coffee drinker and not in demitasse cups that held the very strong coffee as made by Cubans. Later, I learned to almost like it and found that coffee laced with a substantial amount of hot milk was more to my liking. It was with regret and misgivings that I left the Welfare Department and the Cubans in September of 1971 to return to Purdue.

My Purdue mentor was aware that I was married and the mother of five children. In addition to encouraging me to continue with my education, he also helped to ease the financial pressure making it possible for me to continue with my studies. From September 1971 to June 1973, I was employed by Purdue as a graduate assistant in the Psychology Department. From 1973 to 1974 I continued to serve as guest lecturer in the General Studies Program. Work on my master's ended on June 11, 1972, when Perdue awarded me the Master of Science degree in education. Still this mentor was relentless and encouraged me to strive for a PhD. I applied to several universities and awaited their reply. In the meantime, I looked for a job.

Before exiting from my discourse about Purdue, I am compelled to say that beginning my college experience in its small square two-storied building, with the cafeteria in the basement, was a boon for students. The cafeteria was the place where faculty and students could mingle and interact with each other. It was not unusual to note the mixture of professors and students sitting at the large round tables. It was a time for the free exchange of ideas without the penalty of censure! How was it possible that I, an American of Mexican ethnicity, was privileged to mingle with and exchange ideas with the highly degreed professors who were our instructors? And I did!

# 35

The 1970s brought sorrow to the Lopez families, beginning with my father's death. Luis's family was shocked by his sudden death on January 4, 1971, six months short of his eighty-fifth birthday. The previous day, Rudy, our five children, and I were returning home from Chicago, where we had visited my brother Joseph and his family. The ice and snow on the highway were treacherous. When we were about fifteen miles from home, the car skidded and struck the guard railings. The car was not seriously damaged, and we continued on our way. Shortly after arriving home, we received a phone call notifying us that my father was in critical condition. He had fallen as he was shoveling snow. He was unconscious and was rushed to the hospital in Blue Island, less than a block away. Because of the severity of the weather and condition of the roads, it was impossible to travel to Blue Island. Early the next morning, the roads were passable, and leaving the children with Rudy, I drove to the hospital. When I entered his room, the bed was empty—my father was dead. Funeral arrangements were made; family, relatives, and a myriad of friends were in attendance at the church and related services.

On December 14, 1973, Manuel, the oldest Lopez brother, died at the age of eighty-six, about two years after Luis. Recalling that he adamantly refused to have one of his badly mutilated legs amputated because of a serious accident, the Lopez families were happy that he was buried wearing two shoes. His wife, aunt Silveria, died on July 12, 1974. Three years after my father's death, Felisa, his wife and my stepmother, who was a diabetic and having difficulty with her eyesight, was hospitalized in November 1974 and subsequently died. She feared blindness and being a burden to her three sons. George Rincon, Rudy's oldest brother, passed away on October 12, 1975. On April 13, 1976, my oldest brother, Walter (Wally) died. At the time, he was hospitalized in the VA Hospital located near the Chicago campus of the University of Illinois. He had been diagnosed with viral hepatitis. I was a student at the university, and visiting him was not a problem. I saw him the day before his death. The university provided me with the injection necessary to combat my exposure to the hepatitis. I can never forget the love and thoughtfulness Wally manifested with his family, especially with his sisters. David Nelson Resler, my son-in-law's brother, died on December 23, 1978. He was struck by a vehicle as he hiked from Florida to his parent's home in Munster, Indiana.

The 1970s also brought other significant changes. It was a time for weddings, a college graduation, a divorce in the Rincon family, and an appointment by Governor Bowen. Our son, Damian, married Mary Kay O'Brien in June of 1973. They were graduated from Bishop Noll Catholic High School but not the same year. Damian was graduated one year before Mary Kay. The nuptials took place in St. Mary's Catholic Church—the church attended by her family. It was a lovely celebration followed by a reception and dancing at a local banquet hall.

In May of 1976, it was with great pride that Rudy and I accompanied our oldest daughter, Marcie, to Purdue University's campus at

Lafayette, Indiana, where she was graduated with a bachelor's degree. She became engaged that year to Steven Resler. Their marriage took place in May of 1977. It was a beautiful wedding in Our Lady of Grace Catholic Church—the church attended by the Rincon family. The reception was held at a restaurant that was built in the middle of a beautifully landscaped wooded area. It was a pleasure for the guests who strolled around the terrain.

An event that occurred on November 11, 1978, was the marriage of our youngest daughter, Wendy, to Michael LaBounty. She was given in marriage by her brother Damian. After a lovely ceremony in St. James Catholic Church, the church attended by both families, a lively gathering of relatives and friends joined the couple at a local restaurant to help celebrate their union. This year, 2010, they celebrated their thirty-second year of marriage.

Rudy and I had decided to delay our divorce until our daughter Marcie's wedding. Ironically, the divorce took place on Armistice Day, November 11, 1978, but not intentionally. Also, we were not aware that it had been granted the same day as our daughter Wendy's marriage. Hence, it did not dampen Wendy and Mike's wedding. Issues relating to the divorce are discussed later.

In the mid 1970s, I was invited by Governor Bowen of Indiana to serve a three-year term in the Governor's Commission on the Status of Women in Indiana—a commission created in the United States in 1946. In the current commission, women from various areas in Indiana comprised the membership of the commission. To be a part of this commission was an honor. The monthly meetings with spirited women were held in Indianapolis with the intent of discussing pressing women's issues around the state.

# 36

As I look back on my employment history, it appears I was always filling a need. In August of 1972, a friend/director of the School City of East Chicago's bilingual program approached me and asked whether I would consider filling the remaining position needed so that the bilingual program would not be delayed or possibly abandoned. I accepted the position, and from September 1972 to June 1973, I was hired as a kindergarten teacher by the School City of East Chicago, Indiana to fill the position. Was I qualified? Educationally, yes, and if one counts the practical experience of having raised five children from birth to their teenage years, I was more than qualified.

It was exhilarating and exhausting to keep fifteen children, four and five years old, in line for the morning session and then repeat the activities with fifteen more in the afternoon. On the positive side, it was rewarding to have the children absorb the material being taught and to note their gains. On the negative side, it was not possible for me to leave the room, even for bathroom use, without the tykes following me. This was at times constricting and made me feel like a mother hen. In the evening I was a guest lecturer at Purdue in the General Studies Program, where the curriculum focused on the training of women, often with little experience outside the home, to be qualified to teach in the day care and Head Start programs. Switching hats from teaching kindergarten students during the day and teaching adults at night was quite a challenge. However, undertaking these two jobs simultaneously was made easier because the material was related. Further, the Purdue program was limited to three evening classes per week, per semester. At the end of my year of teaching little people, I was out of a job because applicants for the bilingual position were available.

The following incident is one that came to mind when I was reviewing and typing the forgoing material. I cannot pinpoint the date exactly, but between the end of December 1972 and the first months of 1973, I received an unexpected phone call from a woman who was a member of a local women's club involved with women's issues. For several years, this club selected ten women from Northwest Indiana, who were considered to be among the best dressed. The question the caller asked me was whether I was available to be a participant in the current year's list. My first reaction was to burst out laughing. The second was to inform the caller that I was not the Rincon she sought, that she actually wanted my sister-in-law, Shirley, who was the epitome of fashion. I gave the caller her name and telephone number. I believed that took care of her task.

A few days later, this woman called again and asked if I was Rudy Rincon's wife, to which I replied that I was. She emphatically stated that I was the one that had been selected. Again, I reacted with amusement and stated that I was never asked to participate in any fashion shows because I was too short. She insisted that I think about participating in their project. I agreed to do as she asked. I pondered at length whether I would be comfortable as a member of this elite group. I arrived at the probability that I was selected as the club's token Hispanic representative. To my knowledge, there never had been a Hispanic woman in their yearly selected pool. After thinking what would be gained by my entry into this choice group, I came to the conclusion that if I did, it was not for personal accomplishment but for what it would mean to the kindergarten children to see their teacher in the newspaper. When I arrived at the school the day after the newspaper had printed the pictures of the ten women selected, I was confronted and surrounded by fifteen excited little people in the morning class and fifteen more in the afternoon class, who recognized me, their teacher. Their faces were beaming. It did not matter why I was the chosen one!

The thought that perhaps my mission in life was to become a filler of positions was given further credence when I was approached by the executive director of the Twin Cities Community Services in East Chicago to fill a newly created position. This was a pilot program, and its continuance was contingent on future funding. From July of 1973 to September of 1974, I filled the position of neighborhood organizer for this agency. The job entailed the following: (1) improving the skills of and assisting the directors in charge of the individual programs, (2) provide input for the neighborhood centers, and (3) to be in contact with the needs of the neighborhood. At the end of the year, to the disappointment of the director, funding was not available. I was out of a job!

# 37

From September 1974 to October1979, I attended the University of Illinois Chicago Circle campus (UICC), where I was enrolled in the doctoral program of the Social, Developmental, and Organizational Psychology departments. I sensed no adverse reactions from the staff and students because of my ethnicity or age. All graduate students had offices assigned to them, often shared with one or two students. Because of the distance I traveled daily and the long day at the university, I generally had snacks. When students visited me in my office, the goodies were shared. The students had a small library in the building for their use. At times money was collected to buy books; I was chosen to be the temporary banker, until the money was deposited in a safe place or books were bought. The trust placed on me gave me a feeling of being accepted by the students.

There was one unfortunate incident that dismayed me. One morning, I briefly stepped out of my office on the third floor, leaving the door open, and went into the office adjacent to mine. I was out of my office less than two minutes, returning quickly because I was expecting a student. Someone seized the opportunity to go through the open door and grab my purse. It was under a chair. The thief then exited the floor through the door leading to the stairwell. When I returned to my office, the first thing I noted was that my purse was gone. After I told my neighbor about the missing purse, both of us proceeded to the exit door. We found my opened purse thrown on the floor. The purse had several separate compartments. All the zippers were open and only the money was taken. The library money amounted to fifty dollars, and my personal money was about sixty dollars. The theft was reported to the university, but there was little that could be done about it. Everyone was amazed at how fast and noiselessly the person rifled the purse and dropped it. It was a daring act, considering that it was not unusual for students to be present at any time in their offices or walking to or from them. Professors, too, had occasion to be on the floor. I felt worse about losing the library money than I was about my loss. The students were sympathetic and understanding, assuring me that I was not to blame for the loss of the library funds. The expected student did not appear for the appointment scheduled for her.

My age and family responsibilities did put limits on being able to interact socially with the students after hours. In this respect, often, I felt like an outcast and out of sync. I did manage to attend one late-afternoon party at one of the students' home and was welcomed by the attendees. It was with regret, but of necessity, that I left the party early, leaving the students to enjoy the rest of the evening. Every Christmas the department had an office party. As I recall, delicious food was prepared by professors and students and was proudly displayed for all to enjoy. It was a day for camaraderie between professors and students.

Professors were available in their offices to help the students when their assistance was needed. However, I was reticent to approach them when I had a problem. The manner in which I was raised, especially being a Hispanic woman, did not encourage me to be forceful but rather to defer to others. Hence, even though I had an appointment with a professor, I sat in the outer office waiting patiently to be called in. I witnessed students coming into the anteroom and going directly into the professor's office. No thought was given to the possibility that someone was awaiting his or her turn. And adding to my uncertainty about the PhD, often, when I met with my major advisor, he would question whether I really wanted the PhD degree. That he felt called to ask me as often as he did caused me to wonder whether he was hinting that I was not fit for or lacked the intelligence to be a student in the department. In 1976, I was granted a position as a graduate instructor in the Educational/Psychology Department of the University of Illinois Chicago Circle campus. This helped with the expenses I incurred, as I commuted daily to the campus from my home in Highland, Indiana.

While at the university, there was an event that affected me deeply. My Purdue mentor suffered a professional loss in 1977. Shortly thereafter, he was diagnosed with cancer. It was devastating to see this robust, healthy man waste away. I was blessed to be able to visit with him and his wife at their home in the days before he died. Once, rising up slightly and painfully from his bed, he looked at me and asked, "Minnie, are you a turncoat too?" His question was not easy to hear, and I assured him that no way could I or would I ever turn against him. He died on July 3, 1979. I attended his funeral. I will never forget this man for the encouragement and help he gave me. After his death, I questioned the value of a PhD.

During my years at the university, I had two publications: the first was written with one of my Purdue professors: Rincon, E. & Ray,

R., Bilingual Ethnic Teachers as an Answer to Illiteracy and Drop-Out Problems – 1974; the second was a sole effort: Rincon, E. L. – Comparison of the Culture Bias of the KIT (Kahn Intelligence Scale): Exp. With the WISC (Wechsler Intelligence Scale for Children) Using Spanish Surname Children Differing in Language Spoken – 1976. After I withdrew from the university, I had two more publications, coauthored by one of my major supporters at UICC, Christopher B. Keys, to add to my résumé, titled The Latina Social Service Administrator: Developmental Tasks and Management Concerns, Administration in Social Work Journal, which was published in spring, 1982. The latter was again published as The Latina Social Service Administrator Developmental Tasks and Management Concerns-An Introduction to Human Services Management, which was edited by S. Slavin and published by The Haworth Press in 1985.

For about five years, I had driven Highway I-94 five days per week from my Highland home to UICC, generally without taking a break between quarters. I left willingly in 1979 sans the PhD for which I had been struggling. I have pondered over why I was willing to give up this coveted goal. The reasons which come to mind are the following: energy waning, daily driving, losing my family in the process, and so forth. Another important issue was whether the relationship of my children and siblings toward me will change or would I change toward them because I had "outgrown them." In all honesty, a thought that I toyed with occasionally and ignored was whether I was fooling myself into thinking that I was PhD material. The ultimate question was would I be losing more than would be gained by having a PhD?

# 38

The summer of 1975, Rudy, my husband, decided to take advantage of the thirteen-week vacation offered by his employer, Inland Steel, to employees who qualified for this awesome benefit. He had a plan we discussed at length. He planned to use six weeks of his vacation to travel through the United States, Mexico, Central America, and Panama using our new Ford Pinto. His end goal was to visit one of our godsons stationed in Panama. He asked me to accompany him. Although I wanted to, I knew that I could not refrain from worrying about our children during our absence. Also, I was not comfortable leaving our children in the care of someone else for that length of time. I declined, believing that it would interfere with our enjoyment and put a damper on his. I was not adverse to his plan to go solo. Knowing how much he enjoyed traveling, I encouraged him in this venture, assuring him that the children and I would manage well. Anyone who knew of his plan was amazed that he proposed making this trek safely through some poverty-stricken and unsafe areas. It did not surprise me that he returned unscathed and full of stories about his adventure. He brought me a gift of a beautiful handmade, tri-colored beaded necklace from Costa Rica. After returning from his trip, he seemed happy, and our life went on as usual. However, I wondered if he thought about our marriage, the life we shared, and my being bent on continuing with my studies. It is likely that he did.

We never brought up the subject nor did we discuss the possibility that there was something amiss in our marriage. Rudy seldom showed displeasure with me, but perhaps I was too busy to note it. I recall only one instance. To this day, I have wondered what triggered the anger he displayed toward me one day while I was on my knees scrubbing the kitchen floor. When he approached me, no words were exchanged, but the look and anger on his face could not be mistaken. It passed. I finished scrubbing the floor and continued to tend to the needs of the family and, of course, attend the classes for which I had registered. As I recall, shortly thereafter, the subject of divorce was brought up by him. I have given a great deal of thought to the issue but can say that at the time I was not considering divorce. I recalled the vow I had made at our wedding before the Blessed Virgin that I would do everything I could to make our marriage work. I, however, did nothing or said anything to argue against the divorce. I could not take back the baggage I brought into our marriage nor did I bring up what I believed was the major issue. I realized that Rudy was not able to handle the issue, and going into therapy was something he would not consider. Perhaps he did not believe in therapy. A thought that occurred to me was that he may have feared that if he did partake of therapy, unpleasant issues about his family might be revealed. However, once he made up his mind on an issue, even one regarding our children, it seemed that he was unable to or could not change his position.

Rudy and I had decided to wait until after Marcie and Steve were married to start divorce proceedings. After twenty-seven years of marriage, we were divorced on November 11, 1978, ironically Armistice Day. It was an amicable divorce and neither one of us ever remarried. In actuality, I never felt divorced. Relatives and friends were shocked about our divorce but more amazed at the friendship we maintained. Most holidays were spent as a family unit. Our children did not have to deal with the ugliness many children endure when their parents are divorced. I did not ask for any of his social security or retirement benefits. He asked for a portion of the home, and he decided on the dollar amount he wished. He willingly accepted that child support was his obligation. After the divorce, Rudy was a generous and a devoted father to his children.

About the time of the divorce, I had the opportunity to invest in a plan that was guaranteeing more than 15 percent interest. I had no money. He did. I offered him this opportunity, and he made the investment in my name. I touched no part of this boon. He kept it in my name until he was ready to take it over, investing it in a plan of his choice. Financially, he did very well with it.

Regrets? I can honestly state that I have had them. I never went into marriage with the idea that if it did not work, I would get a divorce. Perhaps I could have been proactive in trying to save the marriage. Would giving up my educational involvement have helped? A sincere wish by both of us to work on the marriage did not materialize and might have given our marriage a chance! A regret I do have is that we did not take the time to discuss, to some extent, our intent to divorce with our children and some personal issues that were involved.

# 39

Rudy and I were both culpable in terminating our marriage. It was not easy for me to address what I believe may have been at the root of our problem. The reader will recall the issue discussed above about the sexual abuse I suffered, one of which I had no knowledge of why or what had prompted this man's behavior, or why any man would put a young child through this terrifying experience. At age eleven I was totally ignorant of sexual issues. I realize now that subconsciously I completely shut down that aspect of my development. Much later, I recall occasionally saying somewhat boastfully to a few female friends and later to my therapists that, "south of the navel I don't exist." I am clueless as to whether I was aware of why I made the statement or what I meant by it. No one ever questioned what I was saying or why I was saying it. Would my therapist's questioning the statement been helpful? When I married, I was totally ignorant of what was in store for me. Also, Rudy, too, was not the man about town that, given his handsome looks and personality, he could have been and was not. No one sought to give me advice or talked to me about marriage. Actually, we were both neophytes on the issue of marriage.

I have mentioned that I was an avid reader and must have come across material related to married or unmarried couples and sex. I can recall reading terms such as "cold" and "frigid" and firmly avow and believe that I blocked out material of that nature for reasons, at the time, not known to me. Because I welcomed, enjoyed, and initiated being hugged by male and female members of my family and friends, I never related the terms "frigid" and "cold" to me. I do not know whether in these instances, "my feelings stopped at the navel." When I told Rudy about the molestation mentioned earlier, he had difficulty understanding why therapy was needed to help me with the problem and why the molestation affected me in this way. I had no clue that I had been damaged by the experience in a way that it would affect my marriage. I do believe that therapy could have been the answer with participants, who are willing to endure the pain that is likely to occur. It would require that the couples be supportive of each other.

Rudy was not alone in his confusion about the problem. Most men, who marry sexually abused women, have difficulty handling and dealing with this extremely personal issue. In my case, I ask that my pre puberty age and being totally ignorant insofar as sex was concerned at the time of the insult to my body be taken into consideration. As I wrote the words "cold" and "frigid," I was hit hard as I applied their meaning to me.

After the divorce, I had no desire to join the singles world. Marcie, my oldest daughter, was concerned that I was staying at home too much. One evening she visited me with the intention of getting me out of the house. She suggested we go to a nearby Holiday Inn restaurant, where a trio provided music for dancing albeit the area for dancing was small. Knowing that she was concerned about me and wanted to help, we did go to the Holiday Inn that evening and enjoyed the music for a few hours.

# 40

Hearing the live music at the Holiday Inn and my love of dancing prompted me to investigate two ballrooms in the Chicago area about thirty to thirty-five minutes from my home. Music was provided by big bands, generally comprised of ten musicians. These two ballrooms became my outlets for socializing with both sexes.

Glendora on Harlem Avenue was the first ballroom I visited. It offered dancing on Friday evenings. It was there that I met the man who was my companion for more than twenty years. As I saw this man crossing the floor diagonally toward where I sat with friends, I had a strange feeling that he was coming to ask me to dance. He did! Through the years, we parted occasionally, but the parting was always brief. He was a French Canadian citizen and a longtime permanent resident of the United States. He lived and worked in the Chicago area. He also frequented the second ballroom, Willowbrook, on Archer Avenue. There dancing was offered on Thursday evenings and Sundays from 2:00 p.m. to 8:00 p.m. It was next on my list. After that, we spent weekends together dancing on Fridays and Sundays and often saw each other during the middle of the week. He was considerate, caring, and never failed to remember special days with a lovely gift or flowers.

My friend introduced me to Canada and to his myriad of relatives on the East Coast. Windsor had been the only Canadian city I had visited, and with him, I became acquainted with Quebec, New Brunswick, and Prince Edward Island, where he had many relatives. He traveled to Canada two or three times each year and generally asked me to accompany him. His relatives always welcomed me warmly. I will always treasure the visits with his relatives and feel blessed to have had this intimate exposure to many Canadian people and their country. I will continue with the relationship with my Canadian friend further on in this manuscript when I deal with incidences occurring between 1996 and 2004.

# 41

I am puzzled as to why I am reverting again to the molestation issue. Did my return to dating have anything to do with it? Does it have any connection with the fact that as a school psychologist and as a therapist for a psychiatrist, I had occasion to work with children who had been molested? Or perhaps it is because of an outcome from my participation in a week's training in hypnosis in the 1980s in Chicago and, in 1990, attending a workshop held in Michigan City, Indiana, addressing child and adolescent sexual abuse. I lean toward the hypnosis and the workshop experiences as major influences in bringing to light the possibility of being molested as a young child.

The possibility first came to light in the mid-1980s, when a coworker and I, both school psychologists, attended a week of training in hypnosis in Chicago. The seminar was limited to master-level professionals. When the instructor asked for a volunteer to be a subject, I raised my hand. For some reason unbeknown to me, I was on the verge of tears. He asked if it was okay to touch me on the knee. I responded that I did not mind. In the hypnotic trance, he (regressed) brought me to my birth. When age two or three was reached, I broke down sobbing profusely. The hypnotist was very attentive to me, speaking softly as he worked at calming me. As I opened my eyes and looked out at the hypnotist trainees, I noted that my breakdown caused several of the attendees to tear, my coworker included. Softly and gently the hypnotist questioned why I had broken down at that point. I responded that I was confused; I did not know and was unable to give him a reason. At the end, he said that I had more work to do. He was right. Although my mother had died when I was four, I was positive it was not the reason for my tears.

Then years later, on February 12, 1990, I was one of many working in the field of psychology who attended a workshop at a hospital addressing child and adolescent sexual abuse. The main focus was on a professional female, who worked with abused children. She portrayed the role of a very young female child who was molested, continuing the portrayal to include adolescence. She began by being dressed as a baby, wearing a bonnet as worn by infants and carrying a bottle. As she proceeded through her presentation, she changed some of her clothing. From the onset of her presentation, I felt extreme anxiety, at times holding the armrests tightly. I held back tears, hoping that the coworker seated beside me, and one with whom I had a close relationship, would not notice my discomfort. This coworker and I had attended the hypnosis training noted above. It took great resolve to sit through this woman's portrayal of an abused child. The audience was somber and very quiet at the end, suggesting that many in the audience, too, had been deeply moved. I wondered how many women in the audience related to the child depicted. It has been reported in the literature that infants have been subjected to sexual molestation.

From that experience I could not let go of the feeling that I may have been molested between the ages of two and three. To give credence to this feeling is that, in later years, whenever I came across this unnamed perpetrator, a person whom I was unable to avoid totally, I experienced revulsion. I sought my personal therapist to explore this possibility. At the end of a lengthy session, after I had given her information about the suspected individual and my experiences above, she concurred with me that there was a strong indication that I was not remiss in my contention of having been molested as a very young child.

When I returned home from the presentation of sexual molestation, that evening I was compelled to write a letter to the presenter, commending and thanking her for her delivery. In my letter I poured out my experiences to her and what havoc it had caused in my adult life. In my letter, I pointed out that in addition to being molested between the ages of ten or eleven, I may have been molested between the ages of two and three. The presenter's response to my letter was comforting and encouraging. In addition she gave me helpful suggestions, including reading matter and referrals—aids that would help the healing process.

On April 14, 1990, Holy Saturday, continuing through April 15, Easter Sunday, I forced myself to write about how I was still affected by the sexual abuse. The task was not completed without tears. It is a six-page documentary. It is likely that anyone reading this paper will not have doubts as to the damage that is done by sexual molestation.

As I write about these experiences, I have had to accept that I was a frigid wife, and perhaps this was the reason behind my divorce. My wish is that husbands, male companions, and especially therapists, who may be called upon to deal with this problem, would be gentle and understanding and accept that the molested child was not a willing participant in the act. The latter applies equally to any woman or male who has had to endure sexual molestation. Joint counseling is highly recommended for success in dealing with sexual abuse. Counseling is not a quick fix and requires patience and commitment on the part of the parties involved to deal with the pain that goes with the healing.

I have not researched the literature as to the reasons why some males are reluctant to consider therapy as an answer to personal problems, such as the one under discussion. Therefore, what I offer is my opinion. I suspect that, in their minds, it may cast doubt on their maleness or manliness. Or past personal issues, likely to cause grief, may surface; and it is best they remain undisclosed.

Exposing me in this paper has been a freeing experience and perhaps will finish the healing process. In memory of my Purdue mentor, I won't let myself continue living with the nightmares and being "half a woman." I wish to impress on the reader and state vehemently that women who have had to deal with this label did not choose to be frigid. An alternative some use is to resort to prostitution, self-mutilation, or turn to alcohol or drugs. I believe that, at times, to save oneself from the torment about the violation, the subconscious takes over, as in my case, and blocks out the experience. Yet, although it may be buried deep in the subconscious, it is still alive.

# 42

The following section deals with my employment after leaving the University Of Illinois Chicago Campus (UICC). In June of 1978 I was approached by the executive director of the SER, Jobs for Progress agency in East Chicago, to apply for the position she was leaving. She had been offered and accepted a higher-level position with a local steel company. SER was one of over ninety such entities throughout the United States. The outgoing director and I would be the only females to have held such a position. The goal of the agency was to train and locate available jobs for those enrolled in the program. The majority of the enrollees were of Hispanic background, so my bilingualism was an asset. I applied for the position, met with an all-male Hispanic-governing board, and was accepted as the new executive director. For this Hispanic-governing board to have hired two women as directors, in succession, is notable in that it may indicate that Hispanic males were expanding their view of the role of the Hispanic woman. She can be more than mother and housewife.

In this agency, the field trainers and office staff were Hispanic. It was a novel experience for me to be in charge of a Hispanic workforce. I had negative experiences with two female employees that caused me grief. One employee, during a staff meeting, rudely challenged my authority on issues with the underlying criticism being that I had little knowledge of how to run the program or the office. Later, a loyal employee suggested to me that the negativity stemmed from the fact that a male, who was a friend and had worked in the program, was the staff's preferred choice for the directorship. She was not happy with the board's choice. Nonetheless, I realized I had to affirm my position, and in the process I lost a valuable employee. I fired her for insubordination, at which point she went to her office and prepared to leave. I followed after her, stated that I may have acted in haste, and told her to resume her duties. She would not be mollified and walked out. This employee, about two months later, called to ask if she could return to the job. The job had been filled. In the second case, the bookkeeper had erred, presumably intentionally, on the salary schedule of the coming year's budget. The agency's accountant was aware of her error. This employee soon learned that I, too, was aware of her error. I informed her that in the future her work would be examined closely. She remained on the job. Henceforth, this employee was careful but subdued.

In hindsight, the antipathy I felt from some of the female staff was perhaps jealousy about my academic background. This notion is derived from my knowledge of the position of women in the Hispanic culture. Many men, generally, do not approve of a Hispanic female's aspiration for higher education. I resigned the position in April of 1979 because I did not think it was meeting my needs. Further, I was not using the skills or knowledge I had gained with my educational background. To the delight of most of the staff, the position was soon filled with the favored male.

From January of 1980 to August of 1980, I was employed as an immigration consultant by a Chicago law firm, whose focus was to assist immigrants wishing to become permanent residents or citizens of the United States. My bilingualism was a major factor in this position because many of the clients were of Spanish backgrounds. I also worked with English and limited-English clients. This job expanded my knowledge of the world. I interviewed people from more than thirty countries, among which were countries heretofore unknown to me. Employers and the staff worked together closely, and I was impressed with the lack of pettiness in the office. The lawyers made themselves available to their assistants to explain legal issues of which they were not sure and backed the office staff as necessary.

I left the law firm in August because a job as a school psychologist might be available. It appeared to me that finally I could use my education in a setting wherein I could be of service to children with academic or physical disabilities. Also, an important plus, since I was self-supporting, I would benefit professionally and financially from my formal education and begin a retirement "purse."

In truth, I can avow that to date I have enjoyed every job I had. Some of the experiences and learning I had could not be gained from textbooks. My experiences in the practical world complemented my formal education. My formal education had given me the backbone, tools, and knowledge I needed to meet unexpected circumstances. Every job I had, I left with a heavy heart but with good feelings about the staff and the people with whom I came into contact. Except for the two negative SER experiences above, to my knowledge, my relationship with every individual with whom I worked was free of discord or backbiting.

Death did not take a vacation during the 1980s. On March 17, 1980, Uncle Manuel's youngest son, Erie, died and his oldest daughter,

Paula Garcia, died on July 17, 1980. Paula's son Ronald died in December of 1950 when he was in the hospital for a tonsillectomy. Jesse Bustamante, Mary's husband, died on July 12, 1980. On May 8, 1981, my youngest brother, Joseph, was buried. His death was unexpected, as he had always been in good health. My sister Joan, who lived in Mexico, died in May of 1984. Her death was followed by the death of my cousin Leonard, Benito's son, on October 2, 1985. My oldest sister, Cecilia Rangel, who had been ill for several years, was buried on May 3, 1989. She was the mother of fourteen children, still living and on hand to bury their mother. Cecelia's grandson, David Rose died July 27,1975 - felled by a car.

Life goes on. A happy event was that my daughter Judy was married to Charlie Burley on September 29, 1985. Their union took place at Gloria Dei Lutheran Church. The reception was held in Dyer at the restaurant and lounge owned by Charley and two friends. Relatives and friends enjoyed the festivities and dancing to the live music that followed.

# 43

In August of 1980, upon the suggestion of a former Purdue classmate, I applied for the school psychologist position advertised by a large special-education corporation. The supervisor with whom I interviewed was impressed with my credentials and my bilingualism. He pointed out, however, that I would be required to serve a school psychologist internship for one year and complete a required course—Reading Diagnosis. These deficits could be remedied at Governors State University in Park Forest, Illinois. The salary would be $7,000 less than that earned with the law firm. I tend to be prudent and believed I could handle the loss in pay.

I accepted the position and registered at Governor's State University to complete the deficits in my résumé—Reading Diagnosis and Independent Study: School Psych Internship for the fall 1980 term. On July 15, 1983, the transcript from the university indicated that I had completed the requirements to assure my qualification for the position. I joined the employees' union, and in a few years I was selected to be the union representative and saddled with the responsibility of handling employee concerns as well as negotiating new contracts. This was a position that I had never sought or anticipated, but I was pleased that the members had faith in my ability to handle the requirements of the job. I believed that I had finally found the occupation in which my educational training could be used and one that would be rewarding in many ways.

For the first seven years of working for the special education corporation, my assignment was three pronged: (1) the preschool program, (2) a school district in a low income area with a large Hispanic population, and (3) assessment of the educational deficits of Hispanic students in the ten school districts covered by the corporation. Respective to the preschool program, the duty of the psychologist was to assess the abilities or deficits of preschool children, soon to be three or already three to about four and a half years of age. The intent of the assessment was to determine whether the deficits identified in the evaluation would meet the requirements for special education in the preschool program. After completion of the evaluation, a meeting with the preschool teacher, the parent, and sometimes the supervisor was held so that the psychologist could discuss the results of the evaluation. If other professionals—for example, the speech/language and occupational/physical therapists—were involved in the evaluation, their input, too, was required at the meeting. Respective to the second component, students whom the teachers identified as having difficulty with grade-level material were referred for an educational evaluation. The third component of my assignment was to evaluate Spanish-speaking or bilingual students in any of the schools serviced by the corporation of whom teachers had documentation to support the need for the extensive and costly evaluation.

The assignment to the preschool program was a boon because it complemented the previous positions I held. Carrying out the assessment of the strengths and weaknesses of the three- to five-year-old tots referred for evaluations was challenging and sometimes grueling. At times, it was not easy to keep their active behavior at a level so that focus would be kept on the verbal and nonverbal tasks presented. I assumed this assignment enthusiastically, knowing that gaining the confidence and attention of the tykes was important in obtaining a valid assessment.

The district to which I was assigned had a high referral rate; and some students, after being evaluated, were found ineligible for special education because their problems generally stemmed from inappropriate acting-out behaviors. This is a category not covered by special education. The principal and teachers involved, of course, were disappointed in the conclusion that such boys did not meet the criteria specified by law to receive special-education services. I was not oblivious to the difficulty of teaching, especially when a teacher must stop instruction in order to deal with misbehaving children, generally males. I wanted to do something to allay their disapproval when a student referred for an educational evaluation did not meet the guidelines for special intervention. A plan that I had in mind required a second person, preferably one who was knowledgeable in the difference between boys that were acting out from those that had emotional issues.

The coworker I approached to work with me was enthused with the idea of meeting one day per week for an hour for eight weeks with six boys from grades five and six. The focus was on instructing the acting-out boys on the difference between feelings and aggressive behavior. The coworker was in charge of the emotionally handicapped program and knowledgeable about the difference between the two categories. Both of us met with the principal, teachers, and parents involved and presented our plan to which they reacted favorably.

Identification of six of these lads was made easier because some had been referred for an educational/psychological evaluation and found to be ineligible for special intervention.

The core of our intervention was to develop the boys' understanding of the differences between appropriate and hurtful behaviors. To do this, index cards were used on which printed words were connoting feelings, such as love, like, smile, help, and words connoting hostility, such as anger, hate, sneer, and kick. The boys selected a word and then acted it out. Although the boys were glad to get out of the classroom, the first meeting was received unenthusiastically, and it was not easy to keep them focused on the task. It was soon obvious that the boys had little experience with or paid attention to feeling words. Their role-playing with the feeling words was not noticeably different from the acting out of hostile words.

It took about three weeks of working with the boys before they caught on to the nature of the task and learned the difference between the categories of the words. Initially all words were acted out in a hostile or angry manner. At the end of eight weeks, the boys were reluctant to quit and asked if we would continue working with them. We extended the project for two more weeks. At the end of the two weeks, they asked if we would resume working with them if they misbehaved again. Not so dumb were they! A second positive side of the plan was that the teachers involved noted a change in their behavior, and some did better in their schoolwork. The boys enjoyed immensely the unanticipated treat at the end of their hard work—pizza at the local pizzeria, for which a friend had provided some funds.

# 44

The school district to which I was assigned had a bilingual program geared to provide service to parents and students of Hispanic ethnicity and to mingle in the community to get a grasp of their unmet needs. A major concern was the depressed academic achievement and high dropout rate of this group. The directors of the program, heretofore, were not Hispanic. Hence, when the position was vacated and the incoming director was a Spanish-speaking Hispanic working on his doctorate the community was pleased. The high dropout rate among Hispanic children was a concern to me, and I was gratified to be in a position that could have a positive impact in reducing the dropout rate. Often Hispanic students were not referred for an educational evaluation because teachers sincerely believed that the problem was rooted in their background or language spoken at home. Yet Hispanic students have been known to have dyslexia, speech/language problems, or are significantly below average ability. It was my belief that it would be beneficial to have a director who was able to communicate with the Hispanic community. When I met him, I welcomed him and offered to assist him if he had concerns about a student.

The possibility that some Hispanic children, who were functioning below grade level, were not being referred for an educational evaluation because of their ethnicity or language spoken in their home became a personal concern for me. My son Mark, the father of two boys, received a letter from the school asking him to attend a conference scheduled to discuss his son's end-of-year progress and placement for the coming year. My son asked me to attend the meeting with him. In essence, his son, a fourth-grade student, was being denied promotion to the fifth grade because of his inability to master the required fourth-grade material. His father stated that he had no knowledge that he was having trouble in school. I, too, was surprised because I had a close relationship with this fourth grader and his younger brother, who was enrolled in the kindergarten class for the fall term.

I informed the school personnel in attendance at the conference that when the two boys were in my company, I was impressed with their ability to manipulate materials, put objects together, and draw intricate figures. Both boys, however, did not show an interest in books, reading, or enjoyed having someone read to them. The Spanish language component was ruled out because neither boy spoke it. English was the only language spoken in their home. As a school psychologist I had test materials on hand. About a year earlier, I had presented a nonverbal instrument to the fourth grader. With this test, each plate (page) had four different pictures. The tested need only point correctly to the object named by the examiner. Language is not required and no help or clues are permitted. This student scheduled for failure scored in the superior range. I presented this information at the meeting and nothing was decided. I was certain that if the fourth grader was having difficulty with grade-level matter, it was not because his intellectual level was significantly below the average range.

A letter was written to the principal requesting that the fourth grader and the kindergartener be evaluated. The request was honored and testing of the two boys was completed. Their profiles resembled that of dyslexic students. Their full-scale score (verbal and nonverbal tests combined) of the two boys was in the average range. Further, the verbal score was in the average range. The latter was a surprise to the school staff because, generally, in the profiles of Hispanic students, it is noted that the verbal score is significantly lower than the nonverbal component. It is my suspicion that the fourth-grade grandson was not referred for an educational evaluation because of his Spanish surname. The results of the evaluation indicated that my two grandsons were dyslexic and qualified for special-education services. In addition to the special attention provided by the school, I worked with them on their weaknesses daily after school and sometimes on Saturdays and through the summer months. Often, it was not unusual for me to return home at 8:00 p.m. or later. One day per week, a family friend, Jean, assisted with the tutoring. The special-education services and the extensive/intensive tutoring at home proved fruitful. However, most of the credit goes to my grandsons because never, and I mean never, did they refuse to work with Jean or me or to do extra work. Their father reinforced Jean's and my effort to work on his sons' scholastic deficits, and he is to be credited for the fact that his sons were not behavior problems and their school attendance was excellent. The effort on the part of all paid off. The potential failure at fourth grade will be graduated from high school this June of 2011 with his classmates. The kindergarten student has kept up with his class and has surpassed some of his classmates in some areas. This year, 2011, he is expected to be in the eighth grade. I was determined that these two Hispanic students, my grandsons, would not add to the high dropout rate recorded for Hispanic children!

# 45

I return at this point to the bilingual director who informed me that he was in the process of writing the proposal to continue the funding for the coming year, adding that he might need help with it. He added that it would be a plus if the proposal noted that the district had a Hispanic, Spanish-speaking school psychologist. He asked for my résumé and for permission to use it in the proposal. His request was granted. When he approached me for help with the proposal, I told him that it would have to be after school hours because it would not be seemly for me to do work on my employer's time. I did not feel safe being in the school at night nor did I wish to work in his home, which was close to the school. Believing that the best and safest place to work would be my home and having no misgivings or any unpleasant premonitions, I suggested my home as the workplace. He was given the address and directions.

The director raised no objections and the date and time was set. He arrived at the stated time, and after greeting him, I offered him a cold drink. I filled two glasses with ice cubes and Coca-Cola. We sat at the kitchen table, spreading out the materials he brought: a prior proposal, a rough draft, and notes. I had prior experience writing proposals, and with the old proposal as a guide, I believe the new proposal was completed in a few hours. I say "believe" because the only thing I remember after that was the sense of being lifted up from my chair and then having the feeling I was being carried down a hallway. From that point I recall nothing except waking up the next morning in a bed in the spare bedroom, fully clothed. I was bewildered and questioned what had happened. I was aware that I had to get ready for work. When I went into the kitchen, the table was completely cleared of any paperwork and glasses. It was devoid of evidence that work had been completed the prior evening. I can attest that I did not clear the table of the materials on it.

I am firm in the belief that this man put something in my drink to incapacitate me. In the school setting, I tried to avoid him. However, on the occasions when our paths crossed, I cringed and had to deal with the disgusting eerie feeling I felt. It was impossible for me to completely avoid meeting him in the schools' surroundings. When by chance our paths crossed, I turned away. He made no effort to speak to me. Because there was no evidence on me or the bed on which he placed me, I firmly believe that although he violated my body, he may have chickened out and did not carry out the nefarious behavior he may have had in mind. How does one deal with a situation such as this? This one tried to forget the incident. How does one explain what happened? Inviting him to my home to work on his proposal did not include taking liberties with my body!

What goes on in the head of someone who has this experience? I blocked out the name of the scoundrel. The shame to the family, the district, my employer, and the Hispanic community if this were made known would be intolerable to the recipient of this heinous act. Soon thereafter, it was fortunate that I was assigned to another district and would not have to deal with this individual unless a meeting required his presence to assist with a Hispanic student. It never occurred.

Through the grapevine, I learned that this man had left the district during the night without a formal resignation. He left his office in a mess. No one knew of his whereabouts. I may have been able to block out this perpetrator's name, but the incident nagged at me. This was a man who was in the field of education and might have contact with children. I knew the person who replaced him. Shortly thereafter, she left that position to accept the bilingual directorship at a nearby city. I called her to ask for the name of the individual she replaced. She stated that she could not come up with his name at the moment and followed that with, "Why do you want to know?" I told her that he asked for my help in writing the proposal for funding, which, at my suggestion, we worked on in my home. After we finished, I felt myself being picked up and carried along a hallway. He must have put something in my drink to knock me out and carried me to a bedroom. She was quiet and then said, "Minnie, let me sit down. I'm going to throw up." I added that I did not believe he carried out his intent. Something stopped him. Was it the telephone or the doorbell ringing? Or did the framed photograph of my five children hanging on the wall cause him to rethink his intent as he carried me down the hall?

My informant recalled the person, but it took a few seconds before she was able to give me the name, which I am withholding to protect myself. She added that when she took over the position she noted that he was inept at writing a simple letter and wondered how he managed to come up with a well-written proposal. She realized now that it had been with my help. In addition, she gave me information about his overall unprofessional behavior, which I deem is beyond the scope of this paper. Now that I knew his name and that he had been a resident of San Antonio, Texas, what recourse was open to me? I do have relatives in that city. I wish to add here that I could have saved myself the trouble of asking the aforementioned person about this man's name if I had thought to look through some of my personal files. Much later, to my surprise, I found copies he had given me of several pieces of mail addressed to him and from him. None were to or from me. Perhaps in telling this bilingual director, it was my way of alerting someone about the surreptitious character of this man.

Shortly thereafter I visited my relatives in San Antonio. I told my cousin Lupe, with whom I have a close relationship, about what I had endured at the hands of this man. Other than the person who replaced him after his mysterious disappearance, it was the first time I had told anyone about this experience. She was appalled and sympathetic but questioned how I could have gotten myself into a situation such as this. At any rate, we looked through her phone book and found two males with the same name. However, without a social security number, there is little one could do to locate a person. My concern continued to be that this man may still be in the field of education and whether his interests extend to children was not known. I realized and accepted that there was nothing I could do to stop him from committing further crimes of a sexual nature. I let the matter rest but was unable to let his unwanted behavior toward me die.

An unpleasant task that I felt to be my duty to bring to the attention of the principal of the school and the corporation's administrators was the overall inappropriate behavior of a special-education teacher noted by the teaching and office staffs. Her behavior seemed inappropriate in a public school and in the classroom. I, too, observed her unusual behavior, and believing it to be in her best interests, the administrators were informed of it. It is enough to state that I was impressed with the concern, support, and empathy shown by the school district and the cooperative's administrators on her behalf. It is not necessary to cite the nature of the behavior in question.

I have mentioned above that often I sense when a mishap or an unfortunate incident may occur in my life. One day upon leaving one of the schools in this district, I felt a strong urge to stop for gas on the way home. Although my tank was about half full, I stopped at the nearest station. I was appalled when I lifted the door to the gas tank to see debris in the form of dirt, grains that resembled sugar, and leaves. Instinctively I knew that a person or persons had tampered with my gas tank. I informed the station attendant about the damage to my gas tank. He suggested that I not drive the car until the tank had been emptied of fuel and replaced with untainted material. I gave him the job of doing what was necessary. It concerned me that someone felt so much vengeance and anger toward me to provoke him or her to commit this destructive act. The perpetrator of this act never came to light. Nonetheless, as I reflect on the years I was assigned to this district, I never felt overt animosity or dislike. I felt accepted and never made to feel incompetent.

There is another incident related to this district that needs to be addressed. This involved a first-grade child, whom I had tested and found to meet the requirements for special education. It was a shock when I heard through the office personnel that this little boy had died. It was shortly after I tested him. At the time, I was unaware of what caused his death. His wake was held at a nearby funeral home. As I sat at my desk looking at the files that needed attention, I struggled with the notion of making an appearance at the wake. Thinking that my work would not be going anywhere, I left. As I entered the funeral home, I was taken aback by the mother's painful sobbing—sobbing that could not be quieted by the people who approached her to offer their condolences. Because of the many people surrounding her, I refrained from approaching her immediately and took a seat in the last row.

This mother's uncontrollable sobbing continued unceasingly. It was not easy for me to listen and do nothing. I arose and approached his mother. She recognized me immediately, and as I bent down, I put my arm around her and whispered a few words of comfort. Her sobbing ceased and she calmed down. Then she told me what had caused her son's death. It was a very cold day and he was outdoors playing with a balloon. Evidently he had placed the balloon in his mouth and possibly attempted to blow it up. Somehow it lodged in his throat. He ran into his house crying, wanting his mother to rid him of the balloon. Not able to do so, she called 911, but it was too late to save her son. His mother was tormented because she had been helpless in helping him and to ease the terror her son must have been feeling. The room was stilled, and those in attendance wondered what had been said that soothed this heartbroken parent. I walked away and out of the funeral parlor to return to the work that needed attention.

A few years later, a lady, accompanied by a boy about five years of age, was coming out of a school building which I served. I recognized her as the mother of the aforementioned boy. The boy with her was her son and was an identical image of the son she had lost. I greeted her, and without thinking, greeted this little boy with the name of the child I had tested. This little lad looked up at me and said that it was not his name but that of his brother who had died but that it was okay for me to use it. I was speechless as I looked up at his mother and noted the sadness that appeared on her face. With that picture in my mind, I left them with good wishes for the day and continued on to the next assignment on my list.

# 46

After about seven years with the preschool assignment, an assignment I delighted in having, I was relieved of it. It was assigned to another school psychologist. I was reassigned to a district closer to my home. It, too, was in a low-income, somewhat-impoverished area. This district had an exorbitant amount of referrals for an evaluation to determine whether a student referred had significant deficits, as specified by federal law, requiring special-education intervention. I approached this assignment with a positive attitude and determined to serve the district to the best of my ability. The evaluation of Hispanic students in the ten school districts covered by the cooperative continued to be my responsibility.

I have pondered over the situation I had to endure about three years after being assigned this district. The issue was my handling of the district's concerns respective to special education. Not one principal of the schools in the district had ever given me any indication that I was remiss in providing adequate service to their district or that I was incompetent. Every year, principals filled out an evaluation form appraising the cooperative about the service being provided by the school psychologist assigned to it. In reviewing the material in my personal file at home and the cooperative's files, I did not encounter negative material but did find some letters of commendation.

It was with serious thought that I considered whether I should go into this episode, one that attacked the essence of what I had put my family and myself through in pursuit of higher education. However, on the Saturday morning of October 30, 2010, I woke up from a deep sleep with thoughts of the issue at hand. I firmly believed that this painful experience prevailed in my dreams. Again, I pondered seriously whether or not I should go into this period of my life. I prayed, and the message became clear that I must go ahead with writing about this issue. At this time I must refer to a book in my possession, written in 1991. The title of this book is *Feelings Buried Alive Never Die ...* by Karol Kuhn Truman. The trauma of my experience in this district I tried to bury festered in my subconscious, and my entire being called for the telling of it. Previously I have written that I meditate and have dreams that prepare me for something that I had not anticipated. One might call it ESP. I will not bore the reader with all the details of the myriad of communications between the parties involved. Further, no names will be mentioned. When reference is made to my place of employment, it will be designated as "corporation" or "cooperative."

At this point I interrupted my writing to run an errand. As I drove back, a startling thought came to mind. I, an American Mexican and bilingual, was the only minority in the professional pool of about 145 to 150 employees. To this date, it had never occurred to me that my minority status could be an issue. To date, I never felt antipathy from any of the cooperative's employees, professional and office personnel, nor from those with whom I had come into contact in my previous assignment.

Whether my ethnicity had any bearing on what transpired with the current district may or may not be of relevance, so I let it rest and continue the discourse about what I suspected—probation.

About two years in the new assignment, I felt uneasiness as I moved about the district. Then I began to suspect that my supervisor may have been gathering information, or receiving it, about inadequacies in my performance in the new district to which I was assigned. On March 7, 1990, my supervisor, a school psychologist (a union member), and I met to discuss the complaints against me in an informal setting. Discussion revolved on what constituted complaints. The psychologist assisting me questioned whether the complaints were based on hearsay, names of complainers, or other factors. Because the supervisor mentioned input from kids, he then asked whether it was now a practice for kids' complaints against the school psychologist to be given validation. The questions were ignored. Little was gained at the meeting. I continued working on the numerous requests for psychological/educational evaluations.

To continue with my suspicion about probation, I received a letter dated March 7, 1991, from my supervisor regarding "my job performance with specific areas of concern thus far during the school year." The bottom line was, in my words, there was doubt as to the accuracy of the evaluations I completed on the students referred; and my rapport with parents and students tested was quick, terse, and unfeeling, perhaps cold. The latter troubled me greatly because generally most people found me to be a caring individual. As I was thinking, reviewing, and writing about the charge against my ability to handle the school psychologist position, it occurred to me whether the incident with the bilingual director in my previous assignment had propelled me into developing a protective shell and gave people the notion that I was uncaring as I handled the job. Because of the shame, I had told no one—the school district or the cooperative—about the vile behavior to which I was subjected by the bilingual director. I had put this vile incident behind me so that mentioning it at this time never occurred to me.

It is not the purpose of this paper to explain all the issues that are involved in administering psychological tests. It would be too time consuming and would serve no purpose, but I could and did refute each charge on March 19, 1991. I sent a copy of my rebuttal to all the school psychologists and other individuals in whom I had confidence and would support me. I should not have wasted energy or time on refuting the charges. It is my suspicion that reading my response to the charges or giving attention to them was of no interest to the powers that be.

Interestingly, years prior to 1991, in November of 1984, I received a letter from the director of the cooperative complimenting me for my attendance at evening functions at my previous assignment. In the letter, he stated that I had established excellent rapport with that district. In October of 1987, I received a letter from the director of the Head Start Early Learning Center, located in the present district, commending me for "going above and beyond your duty with a family." Later, this individual became a principal in one of the district's elementary schools. In August of 1992, I received a letter from the new director of the corporation expressing her appreciation for my attendance at a school board meeting and thanking me for taking the time during a busy time of the year. Another positive and welcomed comment stated in a letter dated January 30, 1990, is from one of the cooperative's supervisors thanking me "for the time and effort you put forth" on a hearing. In another case she stated that the individual in charge was "pleased with the preparation you people made for the hearing." On the front of an undated greeting card from the supervisor in question, the following is noted: To (a lone female figure represents the "1,"000,000 and in large letters the words that followed are, "ONE IN A MILLION." On the second page of the card, in hand writing, the date is noted as June 6, 1991. The following is condensed: "... I have never been more impressed with your strength and perseverance ... I'm looking forward to working with you."

Am I missing something? I received the previous communication about three months after the letter dated March 7, 1991, regarding my inadequate job performance!

In a conference on May of 1991 with the principal in the foregoing paragraph, my supervisor, and me, the principal pointed out some good qualities about me but added negative ones that impinged on my ability to handle the job, e.g., I was not skilled enough to identify who will be a good referral for testing and that I had difficulty relating to low-functioning parents and did not give them time to reflect on the results of the evaluations. Yet she stated that I always gave good examples and asked the parents if they understood the information that was given. This principal shortly thereafter, in a private meeting, remarked to me that she hoped that if she ever felt like she was not doing right by the students, she would retire from the job. Was she giving me a message? Was she hinting that I was not doing the job for which I was hired and should resign? I will not bore the reader with further data gathered on the writer being considered as incompetent in carrying out the duties of a school psychologist job.

A month prior, a meeting was arranged by my supervisor to meet with her and a special-education teacher to obtain input from the teacher as to how I could improve my skills in carrying out the duties of the school psychologist's job. An interesting suggestion was that because some parents really experience difficulty in certain areas, one should stay away from naming the problem resulting from the evaluation and to not go into too much detail when sharing the information gathered on his or her child. It is best to discuss the findings in generalities, reduce details, and so forth. Is there not a conflict in the suggestions from the principal above and the special-education teacher? The first believed I don't give enough information; the second, that I not give too much and reduce the details when sharing information. Nonetheless, in a letter dated *March 27, 1991*, I received a detailed plan for improvement based on the weaknesses reported by the present district. I did not receive this letter until *April 15, 1991*.

Based upon a dream, I was not surprised when I was hit with the possibility of being put on probation. I felt as if all I had worked for was being washed away. Fortunately a premonition I had helped prepare me for the axe that was to fall. My supervisor handed me a letter with attachments. I looked at the first page, immediately turned to the last page, and then handed the packet to the psychologist who accompanied me; he was with me for support throughout the entire ordeal. In short, I was being recommended for probation. The meeting over, the supervisor told me to take the rest of the day off. I replied that I wanted to return to work. Her terse, commanding response was, "I'm ordering you to take the rest of the day off." Was I given the day off so that I could go home and lick my wounds? How tough could she get? If I didn't do as told, I would be charged with insubordination, and firing might follow. It was by sheer will that I remained unflappable. I left her office, not with my tail between my legs but with head held high as I passed through the clerical section, whose members, undoubtedly, were aware of what was happening in the closed room.

This meeting was followed up by a formal letter from the corporation's director and cosigned by the director-elect dated April 17, 1991, sent via certified mail. In short, based on the discrepancies in my performance documented in my supervisor's report of February 25, 1991, it became their duty to place me on probation for the 1991–92 school years. Further, deficiencies documented must be corrected within the year, and failure to do so would result in a directive from the board of managers to cancel my teaching contract. Threatening, was it not? Why was there such a hurry to act on putting me on probation? I was given a "plan for improvement" via a letter date March 27, 1991, that I did not receive until April 15, 1991. Was this little American Mexican such a threat to the powers that be?

Strange, I never cried throughout this anticipated ordeal. I was too ashamed to tell my children. What could I do? Was it paranoia to think that I was being set up? Was there a hidden agenda? I was four years short of retirement and self-supporting. Our union was weak and hesitant about how to support me and be successful. Further, it is possible that many of the members were intimidated by what was being done to me and, if they supported me, feared possible repercussions. They felt powerless. How sad! When the psychological staff learned about my plight, they were appalled and disbelieving that this action had been taken against me. Initially, I felt support at the meeting arranged by a few members of the staff to address the issue and to determine how they could help. I sensed cautiousness on their part to take a strong stand possibly because it might affect their status with the corporation. In my opinion, they, too, were intimidated by what was happening to me.

Later, I was told by a loyal friend that a recently hired school psychologist had stated that maybe, "Minnie had done something wrong." I realized then that I would have to undertake my defense without help from my peers. I did not see the profit in pursuing the matter legally because of the length of time and money the process would take. Most important was the fact that in about four years I would be retiring. I considered what the outcome might be, and I believed it more advantageous to follow through with the plan implemented by my superiors for my improvement. *I* was determined to prove that I was qualified and competent to hold the position as a school psychologist. Admittedly, as I entered the schools to perform my duties, I would have to give the impression that I was not threatened by the position into which I had been thrown, act normally and do the job to the best of my ability.

Throughout the entire process, thoughts about what my mentor had suffered surfaced periodically. In spirit, I knew he was on my side. At these times, I would vow to him that I would not let them do to me what had been done to him. This was my mainstay. My mentor, who pushed me through the years I was being educated, again was there for me even in death. For him I decided to do all I could to verify the faith he had in me, that is, that I could when I said, "I can't." I cannot leave out that as I prayed, which was often, I asked God to help me through this trial. A few years ago, I had made it a practice to spend at least a half hour every morning reading the Bible. One morning, as I read the Psalms, one in particular was relevant to my predicament: "Instead of striking back, ask God to take your case, bring justice and restore your reputation" (7:1–6). I related it to the decision I had made. I knew I was not alone and had the best support available to man—*God*.

So based on the plan for improvement, I developed questionnaires to gather information from principals, teachers, parents, and kids, whom I tested, for their input about my progress as a competent school psychologist. A detailed tabulation of my referrals by schools was necessary. The results were given to my supervisor. Following that, I was ordered to cut down on the evaluations completed. This was not an easy task, considering the high volume of referrals I received from one particular district. In reducing evaluations, I was sure to arouse the displeasure of some principals. This had the probability that I would also antagonize teachers and parents, who were anxious to receive attention to their referrals ASAP. I was observed administering the tests to the children and how I presented the results to the parents at parent conferences. In the interest of not boring the reader, it is unnecessary to continue with the implementation of the plan as outlined by my superiors. The mandate to reduce the number of evaluations put me in a "dammed if I did and dammed if I didn't" position!

It is my sincere hope that I have been honest about how I proceeded in carrying out the schedule outlined. As I wrote, I hoped I was not fooling myself into thinking that my behavior was not different than it was prior to the probation.

# 47

On June 10, 1991, my supervisor wrote a two-page report on the progress I had made with the plan for improvement developed on March 27, 1991, commenting on the "good job" thus far. On November 14, 199l, less than six school months later, my supervisor wrote, citing positive observations she had made during this period. In short, rapport with students and my administration of tests were no longer viewed as deficits. It is the professionalism component of the letter that meant a great deal to me. It read as follows: "I would like to commend you for the high degree of professionalism you displayed throughout the time I observed you, both in your discussion of the student with me and with other staff persons." She only mandated that I was to take breaks every forty-five minutes so as to maintain a high level of focus. Considering the number of referrals received from this district, adhering to the mandate would be next to impossible. If kept, I wondered how much support I would receive as complaints from the schools came in. I tried! The ending, "Nice job, Minnie," was music to my ears and to my whole being.

Another communication that was rewarding was in a handwritten note from my supervisor dated June 6, 1991. In sum, although we had not always agreed, she wrote, "Yet, I have never been more impressed with your strength and perseverance." On December 19, 1991, my supervisor, now the assistant director, wrote to the new director that, based on my progress on the plan for improvement, she recommended my probationary status be terminated, as I had met the requirements on the aforementioned plan. Merry Christmas! On January 2, 1992, the new director wrote me, notifying me that she had accepted the recommendation of my supervisor/assistant director to end my probationary status for the 1991–1992 school years. Happy New Year! A comment was added on the progress I had made in such a short amount of time. My Kafkaesque experience was over! The latter refers to a book: *The Trial* by Franz Kafka.

There is much more that I can add, but it would serve no purpose, and it is not in my nature to be vindictive or to point at others' faults in the interest of making me look better. It has always been part of my nature to not spend time or energy being angry or being vengeful. If I fought, it was because I believed in myself and in the value my mentor placed on me. I could not, would not, let him down. I will add that I did not look forward to my retirement in 1995 and the party that generally was a part of the process. If it were not for offending some loyal coworkers (school psychologists), I would not have attended. I recall looking out at those in attendance and wished I could read minds. Dr. Elliot, my companion throughout the trial, read his humorous rendition of what makes Minnie tick and lightened the tone of the party. It is a keeper, and I appreciated that he took the time to write it. In essence, I appreciated the opportunity given to me to put my education to use, and I value the years spent in the service of children. To those I may have failed in some areas, or if I offended some along the way, I extend my apology. I know that I left with my head held high and knowing that I had given my best to the work assigned and to the cooperative. I remained in that position from 1980 to 1995, when at age sixty-five I retired.

In 1989 I had learned of a position for a therapist in a firm located in Merrillville providing psychological services. I devoted two evenings per week to this position and do not believe that it interfered with my job as a school psychologist. As a matter of fact, it added dimension to it. If a client did not show up, I had the option of leaving early. When the firm was sold to a psychiatrist, I continued in this employment. A few years later, the psychiatrist relocated to his newly built office in Valparaiso, and I continued commuting to that city. I worked for the psychiatrist for about eight years, retiring because of the difficulty I had driving east with the sun in my eyes in the morning and traveling west in the evening. Working in this field was rewarding but not without its painful moments, as I listened to the distressed lives of my clients. An added bonus was that I became acquainted with a therapist, a coworker, whom I respected and with whom I communicated easily. When I retired and needed help with a troubling issue, she made time for me.

# 48

I am going back in time to deal with the following episodes in my life. In 1986, my children's father, Rudy, suffered a heart attack. After partying with a singles group and while driving the group to another event, he stated that he was in great pain. He held the area around his heart. A nurse in the group immediately called 911, and he was transported to the nearest hospital. After extensive examination, he was scheduled for open-heart surgery. His children were devastated because their father had always been in good health. His survival and healing were remarkable. In a short time he returned to his passion—tennis, a sport in which he excelled—and to socializing with the many friends he had. Further, he was alive when our son Mark and his friend Cathy eloped to Las Vegas and were married on July 4, 1990. Their marriage was celebrated about three weeks after their return in the clubhouse that was available to tenants in Rudy's housing complex. Family relatives and friends were invited to fete the newlyweds.

A few days after our son's marriage, a coworker, who had never been west, and I drove to Denver to visit my godmother, Evelyn, and her son, Michael. When my godmother opened the door to greet us, I was appalled by her overall appearance. She looked shrunken, and her face had the look of someone seriously ill. Instinctively, I knew that she was dying. I learned that she had been diagnosed with pancreatic cancer and was given a few months to live. At night, my very considerate friend retired early and left us alone. Nightly, my godmother and I carried on serious conversations. She was deeply concerned about what would happen to Michael. In the meantime, during the day, my traveling companion had fallen in love with Colorado and kept busy making inquiries about vacancies for a school psychologist that might be available or become available. To her delight, there was. She lost no time, and her plans were made to complete the requirements. She was hired for the 1990 fall term. When we prepared to leave, my godmother looked at me sadly and asked if I would come back soon. I instinctively knew she meant ASAP. When I returned home, I lost no time in booking a flight to Denver.

Upon my return to Denver, I learned that my godmother had become a hospice patient, and arrangements were being made for a hospital bed as soon as Michael was placed in the home of a woman who cared for a small number of boys. His mother did not want him to witness the hospital bed brought into his home, which, without doubt, he would know it to be for his mother. In spite of his malady, he was a sensitive person. I remained with her in her home until her condition worsened to the point when she was moved to the hospice facility. There, her daughter Rita and I took turns being with her 24-7. It was with regret that I had returned home on the flight scheduled. My godmother died the next day, July 12, 1990. I thought about Michael and how he was faring without his mother, who had been his constant companion and only caretaker for thirty-eight years.

The following incident is one that must be recorded for the sake of elderly women or of different ethnicities who are hospitalized. Said female may be deeply upset by being cared for by a male attendant. One morning, while Rita and I were visiting her mother, a male attendant entered the room and prepared to care for Evelyn. From her prone position, upon seeing the male caretaker who may have attended her the day before, she sat up and, almost hysterical, said in a pleading voice, "Please, no man." Rita and I instinctively realized, knowing her background and sheltered upbringing, why she was so agitated by having a male attend to her. Her wish and our request that the male be replaced by a female were honored. It saddened us that Evelyn was subjected to this experience when she was near death. However, hospice personnel were not aware that having a male attends to her would upset their patient. This is an issue to be taken seriously by the medical field.

There were other family deaths in the 1990s that intervened to disrupt my life. On April 20, 1990, my brother Joseph's wife, Angela, was buried. Her death was unexpected. She was found on her kitchen floor near the telephone. It was suspected that she was trying to call for help. I drove from my Highland, Indiana, home to her home on Chicago's north side. She was still on the floor when I arrived. Her daughter, Carolyn Lopez, MD, lived a few blocks away and had been on her way to visit her mother. We awaited her son, Robert Lopez, and the undertaker.

In 1991, two of my uncle Manuel's sons died; John on May 23 and Calixto on December 27. Alex Orozco, Marge's husband, died on November 20, 1991. My niece Carmen, Joseph and Angela's youngest daughter was buried on September 14, 1995. On September 17, 1995, a nephew, David Perez, my brother Walter's stepson, was buried.

David was found on the street near his home without identification. It was Sunday, and he had gone out to buy the newspaper.

Years earlier, David and his mother, Margaret Lopez, left Illinois and moved to Fort Lauderdale, Florida. Shortly before her son's death, Margaret had been diagnosed with pancreatic cancer and was given a few months to live. Because she had no relatives, the court appointed a guardian for her, and for her health and protection, she was hospitalized. Hearing of David's death and Margaret's health issues, my sister Mary, her husband, Luis Zamora, and I flew to Florida to be with her. She wanted desperately to be discharged from the hospital to attend her son's funeral and to put her affairs in order. On this first trip, we were able to have Margaret released from the hospital and brought her home. My sister and I had cleaned her house in preparation for her return. And she did attend her son's funeral.

Subsequently, my sister and her husband returned home. I remained with Margaret to give her support as she grieved the death of her son. If she shed tears, it may have been in private because I did not observe any. Occasionally, she mentioned David briefly. Throughout this period and to the end of her life, she was stoic and generally with a smile on her face. Margaret and I spoke at length. To the end, as she did throughout her life, she was looking for ways to augment her income. She was a businesswoman! Looking forward, she spoke about getting together with Mary and me to start a business once the sale of the five apartments she owned was finalized. Suddenly, she became serious and asked in a soft voice if I knew the status of her health. It is my belief she needed to hear it from me. Holding back my tears, I told her that she had been diagnosed with pancreatic cancer. Following that, she asked how long she was given, and with misgivings, I stated that to my knowledge, at the time of her diagnosis, she was given three months. She already knew the information I gave her but needed to have it confirmed.

Mary and Luis had planned on returning to Florida, and when they did, I flew home to attend to some business. It was a blessing that they returned when they did, because shortly thereafter, Margaret's condition was so grave that she was hospitalized. Upon hearing the latter, I made plans to return immediately, but I was too late. Mary and Luis were with Margaret as she was dying. The three of us, her court-appointed guardian, and two of her son's friends were the only ones in attendance at her wake. One of her son's friends took it upon himself to inform the undertakers that internment would follow immediately after the wake, without our presence at the cemetery. We insisted that, however small, there had to be a procession to the cemetery. Her guardian supported us and our wish was granted. It was the smallest, saddest wake and cortege we had ever attended. Three cars followed the hearse: the guardian's, David's friends', and ours.

# 49

I return again to Rudy. About five years after Rudy's heart attack in 1986, he had another heart issue, which was corrected without surgery. His physician did inform him then that there was a possibility he might have another heart problem that would require surgery. The latter was something about which he was adamant. He vehemently vowed that he would never go through that again. Urging and pleading from his children that he consider it fell on deaf ears. He was not about to experience that pain again, and to the end held to his decision. He continued playing tennis and enjoying life with his children and friends.

Around the first of August 1996, Rudy was, according to members of his tennis team, playing as he never had before. He could not be stopped. Suddenly, he fell. At first, his companions did not consider his fall serious until he lay still and unmoving. There was some delay in calling 911. When the paramedics arrived there was difficulty resuscitating him. He was rushed to the hospital. Physicians and hospital staff on hand worked diligently to bring him to a state of consciousness. Our children were devastated to see their father, once a vibrant man, speechless and in what appeared to be a vegetative condition. They were in a quandary as to what was best for their father. The major question was whether to allow the insertion of a feeding tube to keep him alive in the hope that he would return to normalcy, not lose him. Initially, there was no consensus among our five children. I remained an outsider in their decision, believing that it was not my place to influence their decision. Our youngest son, Mark, held firm to not resort to tube feeding, something that his father abhorred. He had spoken to this son and to his doctor that he did not wish to have any extreme measures or tools used to keep him alive.

One day I was visiting Rudy and was the sole visitor. The neurologist entered the room and proceeded to view the EEG. I turned to the specialist saying, "Look at the EEG, it is totally black. It appears that only his primitive brain is functioning. Knowing Rudy, to keep him alive would be inhumane." During this time, Rudy was very restless, agitated, and making unintelligible sounds.

The specialist made no verbal reply, but as he turned to leave the room, he looked at me with sympathy. Because Rudy had talked to our youngest son, Mark, about his wishes regarding his health, his children decided that using the feeding tube was not an option. If used, it would dishonor their father. The medical attendants supported the decision, and he became a hospice patient.

When Rudy was released from the hospital, he was placed in my son-in-law Charlie's mother's home. He was made comfortable in a large room—his bed placed by a picture window. It was not easy to witness his agitation and to hear his unintelligible vocal sounds. It appeared that he wanted to say something—to be heard, understood. So that he would not be alone, his children, extended family, and I took turns 24-7.

# 50

In the meantime, I was faced with a difficult decision. A few months before Rudy's fall on the tennis court, I had enrolled in a week of intensive training in hypnosis to be held in Boulder, Colorado. The seminar was prepaid, and reservations at a nearby lodge for the week were made. Also, my Canadian companion had made arrangements to make the trip with me. We would be traveling by car. Another reason why I wished to make this trip was to see a nephew, Michael, with whom I had a close relationship. He had Down syndrome and was the son of my godmother, Evelyn, who was there for me as a child and as an adult. Her death is noted above. Aside from letting me know that she had given birth to a son on October of 1952 and had named him Michael, she mentioned nothing about his malady.

Perhaps to allay my guilt of leaving Rudy and our children at this time to see Michael, I feel the need to tell his story. In 1956, four years after Michael's birth, I mentioned to Rudy that I would like to take a trip to Denver to visit my godmother. Rudy was always ready to travel. We packed up our three children, ages one, two, and three, and took off. I had called my godmother to let her know we were on our way. When we arrived at her home, we knocked on the door. She opened it, and when she saw us, it was with joy and, as usual, with a smile on her face. I brought Michael a suit size four, his age at the time. When I saw Michael, I was shocked to note his petite physical stature, and I recognized the Down syndrome. It would probably take two years before he would grow into the suit. I noted the anguish on his mother's face, and I hoped I was able to mask the astonishment I felt. A daughter and son, now in their teens, were healthy, normal children. The suit was put away to be worn when he grew into it. Michael was a delightful child, raised with the expectation that he could and would be taught proper behavior. We had intended to make our visit short, and after two days in a motel, we left for home.

I made visits to Denver periodically without my family and saw a well-behaved happy boy with proper table manners, etc. He became very attached to me; often we would be seen with arms linked. He seemed to sense when I would be leaving, and a few days before, he would say, "Minnie, I miss you already." Michael functioned at a very concrete level of thinking. From childhood to adulthood, he never wavered from his delight in watching children's programs and some sports. He learned the numbers of the channels showing his favorite programs and favorite sports. He tuned in to them without help. He kept busy playing with rubber bands, cutting paper, and scribbling. He took no interest in and avoided mechanical toys. Michael seemed to be even tempered and obedient. His mother did everything in her power to provide a happy, stress-free home for her son.

When Michael was twenty-one, his brother Henry died in October of 1973 at the age of thirty-four. His father, Lino, a patient in a hospital in Denver, dressed himself, put on his overcoat and hat, and walked out of the hospital without being noticed. It was December 1978. Lino was well-known in the Denver area. He was reported missing, and there was a general alarm in Denver and neighboring towns about his disappearance. Many weeks later, he was found frozen in a snow-covered field. His date of death was December 17, 1978. After Lino's funeral, I flew to Denver to be with my godmother and Michael. I do not know for certain whether Michael was aware that his father had died. His father's job often required that he travel, and Michael may have believed he would return.

Another tragedy occurred when Michael's mother was doing yard work. She felt something flit across her eyes. She brushed at her eyes, and to her dismay found that it was not an object that obscured her vision but that she had tunnel vision. Whether Michael was aware of his mother's visual impairment is not known. She tried to function as normally as possible to maintain her home and care for Michael. She enlisted Michael's help with simple chores. She color coded dishes and utensils often used and put tapes of varying colors around the kitchen and bathroom counters; thus she made her way around the house without bumping into objects. Mother and son were constant companions and were separated only in times of critical matters. His sister, Rita, who lived in a nearby town, was on hand to help her mother when she had need of groceries, visits to the doctor, or unexpected emergencies. On July 12, 1990, Michael's mother died the result of pancreatic cancer.

The story of Michael is not over. A few years after his mother's death, Rita, his sister, called me to tell me that Michael was in the hospital and was not given long to live. He was on dialysis and was not responding. There was no choice. I left for Denver on the first flight available. Rita and I took turns to be with Michael. I do not know for certain whether he was aware of my presence while on dialysis. He did not die and soon was back in the home of the remarkable woman who had been his caretaker. He was not a child, but because his behavior was still that of a child and not a behavior problem, she welcomed him. I returned home relieved that Michael was out of danger. It was my belief that Michael's problem was undiagnosed depression, the aftermath of losing his mother.

# 51

So I continued to be plagued with whether or not to keep the plans for the Colorado trip. I gave careful consideration to the pros and cons of the situation and, with some misgivings, decided to make the trip. I left but assured that Rudy would be monitored by the hospice staff and receive the medical care required. His children would be on hand to take turns to be with him at all times so that he would not be left alone. I cannot recall whether I had forewarned my children about my scheduled trip, but I gave them all the details and where we would be staying. I told them that I would call them daily, and if they needed me, they could reach me on my cell phone. If necessary, I would take the first available flight home. So with apprehension, my companion and I left for Boulder, Colorado, so I could attend the seminar on hypnosis.

On the first day of the hypnosis seminar, the instructor introduced himself, and then the trainees greeted him and introduced each other. The instructor presented a short history of hypnosis. Then he followed that with two movies of actual patients being treated with hypnosis. The progress they made and the breakthrough into the debilitating trauma that prompted the patients to try hypnosis when other methods had failed was impressive. On the following days, the instructor paired the trainees off to practice on one another.

All went well on the first day as the trainees took their turns to be hypnotists and clients. The morning of the second day proceeded as the first. In the afternoon, after I had practiced with my client successfully, I became the client. I did not anticipate what happened next. It is my guess that my trainee had developed skill in the area of hypnosis. In a few minutes, I broke down sobbing. The instructor and trainees stopped what they were doing, stunned by what had happened. Quickly, the instructor approached me and gently asked what had entered my mind that caused me to break down. Tearfully, I said that I visualized my ex-husband, who was on the hospice program, dying. He excused me from being the client but allowed me to be the hypnotist in training. I did not tell my traveling companion what had happened. I made a call to my children to ask about their father's condition and learned that there was no change. I told them that we were proceeding to Denver for a brief visit to see my nephew Michael and expected to be home within the next two days.

After the end of the morning session of the last day of the training, my companion and I left for Denver. Before leaving for Boulder, I had called Michael's sister, Rita, to let her know that I would be in the Denver area. We arranged to meet for a late lunch at a restaurant of her choosing. She said she would pick up Michael but warned me that he might not remember me. When Michael saw me, much to his sister's surprise, he ran toward me, hooked his arm onto mine, and that was the way we were throughout most of the short visit. On parting, Michael and I looked at each other with deep affection and hugged. It was the last time I saw him alive. He died on January 12, 2001 at the age of forty-eight, outliving three family members. I did not attend his funeral.

# 52

When I returned home from the Colorado trip, I took my turn being with Rudy for a period of the day. Our children were concerned that one of Rudy's younger brothers, Jesse, who lived in California, although having been told about his brother's illness, had not called to find out about his condition. Knowing his brother was in a semi comatose state did not move this brother, with whom Rudy maintained a close relationship, to make a call. Finally, on August 16, 1996, Mark, our youngest son, called his uncle. He informed him that if he was to ever talk to his brother, the time was now. He replied that he did not know what to say. With some prompting and with one of our children holding the phone to their father's ear, this brother did manage to speak to him. Rudy was unresponsive, but it is likely that he recognized his brother's voice. It was a short time after the call that Rudy ceased to exist. I was where I had to be with our children, his older brother, John, and a few close friends as he took his last breath. Following his Mass at St. James the Less Catholic Church in Highland, a reception for family, relatives, and friends was held in the Church Hall. As he wished, Rudy was cremated and buried in Arlington Cemetery in Washington DC.

In December of 1999, three years after the death of his father, I had to deal with the unexpected death of our oldest son, Damian. The Sunday preceding his death, he, his wife, Pat, and their two daughters living in Hanover Park, Illinois, had come to Munster, Indiana, to attend a concert. Damian's niece Jade (a violinist and Judy and Charlie's daughter) and nephew David (an oboist and Marcie and Steve's son) were participants in the concert. Except for me, all sat toward the front of the auditorium. I had a bad cold and chose to sit alone in the last row. Before the concert began, Damian came to where I was seated and stood by me. He seemed very subdued and pensive. We exchanged conversation briefly. I regret that I cannot remember what was said. I did suggest he return to his seat at the start of the concert because I did not want him to catch my cold.

After the concert, my daughter Marcie invited all of us to her home in Munster for some refreshments. I went but soon left for home because I was not feeling well. A short time later, the doorbell rang. I was puzzled and wondering who would be calling so late. I went to the door and was totally surprised to see my son and his family. I asked them in. My son was very quiet but said that they wanted to come by to say good-bye to me. His wife and daughters kissed me on the cheek and returned to the car. He continued to stand beside me, put his arms around me, and kissed me on the cheek. He left. It was the last time I saw my son alive.

After taking some cold medicine, I went to bed at about 10:30 p.m. About 2:00 a.m., I was awakened from a deep sleep by the ringing of the telephone. It was my son's wife, Pat, tearfully telling me to come quickly because "Damian is having a heart attack." The paramedics had been called. I was in shock but told her I would get there as soon as possible. Their house was about fifty miles away, more than an hour's drive. Still in shock, I wondered whether I could drive the distance alone. I knew that I had to get to the bank's ATM machine quickly. Whom should I call to tell them that their brother had a heart attack? I called my daughter Judy and then my daughter Marcie. They were adamant about not letting me drive the distance alone. Judy and her husband, Charlie, decided they would accompany me while Marcie left for Michigan, an hour's drive, to bring their sister Wendy to my home.

When Judy, Charlie, and I arrived at my son's home, we learned that the paramedics had not succeeded in resuscitating Damian. He had been taken to the hospital. We were not familiar with the area and anticipated difficulty getting to the hospital. My mind was fuzzy then, and as I write, it is still fuzzy. Someone knowledgeable about the area drove with us to the hospital. My son was still in the emergency room. I do vividly recall that he was still warm when I touched him and bent down to kiss him. The rest is a blur. I do know that his family had to vacate the apartment immediately.

Fortunately, my son-in-law Charlie and my daughter Judy had an apartment available. In addition, because it was determined to have his funeral in Highland, arrangements had to be made to have his body brought to the chosen funeral home. Then arrangements were made for the wake, service, and burial. Damian worked full time for Home Depot and part-time for a company dealing in swimming pools and their maintenance. The latter had an in-house chaplain, who maintained a very close friendship with Damian. He remained with the family throughout this period. After the service at the funeral home, Damian was buried in St. John's Cemetery in Hammond, Indiana, a city adjacent to Highland. Following the burial, a luncheon was held at a local banquet hall for family, relatives, and friends.

A question plagued me, considering his behavior toward me on Sunday after the concert. Was Damian's last visit to me a premonition of his impending death? I firmly believe it was and that it was a gift from God! He died on December 16, 1999.

Compared to losing my son, probation was a piece of cake. Damian was gone; there is no tomorrow. With the probation, although I felt treated unjustly, I had the opportunity to prove that I was fit for the position of school psychologist. It is interesting to note that writing about the probation did not bring the tears that immediately surfaced the minute I started with the writing of my son's death. It was not an easy time for his wife, Pat, and children, his brother and sisters, his very close friends, and me. There are no words that can convey accurately what is felt by the mourner. I have always had deep sympathy for anyone who lost a child. Now I became acutely aware of the pain that one has to endure. I almost lost my son shortly after his birth, and I thanked God for the forty-six years he let me have him. I will never forget the support Home Depot and the pool company gave to their former employee's family and the chaplain who stood by the family.

As I wrote about my son's death, my thoughts focused on my friend Elsie, who had lost a son and a daughter in less than one year. Her sorrow must have been immeasurable! As it must have been for my cousin Sabina Valadez who lost two sons within six months of each other: Edward died on December 11, 2009 and Richard died on May 10, 2010.

# 53

When I retired from the corporation in 1995, a Hispanic school psychologist was available and was hired to replace me. When I was hired by the corporation in 1980, I believe I was the only bilingual school psychologist in the state. After my retirement, there continued to be a need for bilingual school psychologists in Indiana. As the Hispanic population continued to grow, so did the number of Hispanic students who were struggling with school-related matter.

This shortage of bilingual school psychologists was a plus for me, because, after retiring, I had the opportunity to continue working in an occupation I truly like. The Hispanic population in the northeastern area of Indiana had grown tremendously in the 1990s. By word of mouth or by contact with the board of education in Indianapolis, the schools were given my name. Despite the additional and extensive help provided by the schools, Hispanic students continued to experience difficulty with grade-level matter. Special-education services were available; however, before a student could benefit from those services, an extensive evaluation was mandatory to obtain valid information on the specific areas of need. I was available to about ten school corporations to administer the educational/psychological tests required by law to their Hispanic students. The evaluation was essential in determining whether special education was necessary for some Hispanic students to achieve success in school. Sometimes these trips required driving more than 250 miles round-trip, or more than four to six hours of driving. The driving was tiring, but once I was met by the school personnel, their gracious welcome eased the strain from driving.

The corporations for which I provided the services were grateful that there was someone to attend to the evaluations of their students of Hispanic background, some whose English language was limited or nonexistent. Whenever I responded to their call for help and appeared in their schools, the warm behavior of the personnel assigned to assist me made me feel valued. There is one case that stands out in my mind. It made me feel that I had been instrumental in possibly saving this lad from being one of the many dropout Hispanic students. This student was about ten years old and had repeated the fourth grade. Because he continued to have great difficulty with the grade-level material, repeating the fourth grade again was being considered.

As I administered the tests to this well-behaved, well-mannered student, I was impressed with his quick correct responses to some of the timed material, especially with the arithmetic material. The problems on this test were presented orally, timed, and did not permit the use of paper and pencil. At ten years of age, this student was four points short of reaching the top of the scale. When the testing was completed and scored, I was further impressed with his overall profile. It clearly indicated that the weaknesses observed suggested a learning disability. After dismissing the student, I met his teacher in the hallway. I shared my observations, without mentioning scores, about his student and, at my dismay, at the notion that repeating fourth grade was in the best interests of his student. He was delighted about my comments and remarked that he had wondered about this student because in math, orally, he knew answers quicker and more correctly than any of his peers. When paper and pencil was necessary, this student faltered. His teacher asked about placement in their accelerated math program. Emphatically, I replied, "Definitely." This was an experience I treasured, knowing that perhaps I had made a difference in this boy's life.

A positive aspect to this itinerant job was becoming acquainted with many Indiana cities and towns. The negative side was that sometimes I had to spend evenings alone and wished I had someone with whom to explore the area. This may seem overwhelming to some; however, jobs were sporadic. If more than two students in the district needed an evaluation, I registered at a motel for the evening. I drove to these assignments until 2006. Occasionally, since my retirement at age seventy-five, I have been asked to complete evaluations for some bright non-Hispanic children, who did not have scholastic deficits suggesting special education. The school's concern was appropriate placement for the following year.

# 54

At this point, I return to my relationship with my Canadian companion. For more than twenty years, I had accompanied him on some of his yearly motor trips to Moncton, New Brunswick, his birthplace, where his siblings, relatives, and friends lived. With each visit, the relationship between his relatives and me strengthened, and my fondness for the people grew. I was enthralled with the area and enjoyed visiting the neighboring towns. An unusual phenomenon that the residents and visitors to New Brunswick gathered to view was the tidal bore. Daily, the river reverses its flow in the morning and in the evening. Visits to his relatives on Prince Edward Island were by a ferry. The latter was the only public means used to transport people and their vehicles to and from Moncton to the island. I had read about Prince Edward Island, and now, using the ferry, I had walked on it. What a thrill! The ferry itself was not novel to me. In the past, my family used the ferry to cross the Mississippi River, but to have the experience of using it to reach Prince Edward Island was! Visits to his cousins living on Prince Edward Island were always a special treat. The friendship and love between the cousins was obvious. Today, a nine-mile bridge provides the means to reach the island to and from New Brunswick. The bridge may be faster to service and accommodates the growing population of the area, but the joyful, peaceful trip with the ferry is no more!

Generally, on the way to and from Moncton, we stopped in Montreal, Quebec, to visit a sister with whom I had developed a close friendship. So when he invited me to accompany him in April of 1996, I did not hesitate to accept his invitation and eagerly looked forward to another trip via car. And he, in addition to visiting with his family, looked forward to getting his fill of the lobsters and clams abundant in the area. As usual, it was a fun-filled pleasure to visit his relatives. Before we left Moncton, my friend purchased more than one dozen lobsters to share with friends in Chicago. And so, with the lobsters riding in the back of his van, we began our return trip. We had made many trips to Canada by car and did not anticipate any problems.

On May 3, we left Moncton and headed for Montreal to visit his sister, a distance of 576 miles, which we drove nonstop. We spent two fun-filled days visiting, playing SKIP-BO (a card game), and shopping. I had a bad cold, and on the evening of May 5, I took a cold tablet before going to bed. I was sound asleep when I was awakened by my friend about 2:00 a.m. He liked driving at night when traffic was light. He wanted to get a very early start in the hope of making it to Indiana without stopping. Half asleep, I dressed, helped gather our belongings, got in the van, and we headed toward the 401 highway. Shortly after starting, I fell asleep, confident in my friend's driving skills and familiarity with the road. We had traveled about two hours, and suddenly I was brought out of a deep sleep as the van crashed into the side of a bridge. It appeared that my friend may have fallen asleep at the wheel or had suffered some malady.

Feeling no pain, I removed my seat belt and rapidly exited the car to check on my friend, who, too, was out of the car examining the damage. The front driver's side of the van was severely damaged, and the car was not drivable. Because the accident occurred near Kingston, Ontario, help arrived quickly. A tow truck arrived, and the van was towed to the driver's shop. A kind gentleman from a car rental agency near the repair shop appeared. He escorted us to his agency to help us assess our predicament and to discuss our options. We were too far away from the States and too far away from any of my friend's relatives to phone for help. This gentleman drove us to the Days Inn in Kingston, where we checked in. It was May 6, 1996.

After resting, we thought about our options to return home. Flights to Chicago for two were costly, and in addition, if Kingston had an airport, we would have to find a way to get there. There was another concern. The problem was how to get to the car repair shop to retrieve our belongings and, of course, the lobsters, which, were scattered about the back of the van. I came up with the idea of checking on a taxi service to (1) take us to the repair shop to retrieve our possessions and (2) ask if there was a way one of their drivers would be available to drive us to my home in Highland, Indiana, about thirty miles from my friend's home in Chicago.

Once the taxi company's night-duty person heard of our being stranded and being without means of transportation, a taxi was dispatched to the inn. The driver was very accommodating. He drove us to the repair shop, where he and the repairman helped us get our personal belongings out of the van, including the lobsters, into his company's vehicle. We presented him with the idea of hiring him, or another driver if he was not free, to drive us to Highland,

Indiana. To make a long story short, once the price was decided, he, indeed, drove us nonstop to my home. It was a smooth and delightful trip with this excellent driver, who was amiable and exchanged conversation with us easily. Guessing, it may have taken about ten hours to arrive in Highland. The driver continued his helpful behavior by helping us unload our baggage and bringing it into my house. He refused the coffee offered and stated he would find a motel to rest before returning to Kingston. Except for a fractured rib, I suffered no serious injury. My companion never complained about pain and was soon resuming his daily activities, which included work. He was in good health.

Between 1996 and 2002, we made several trouble-free trips to and from Moncton and Montreal. On November 28, 2002, after a family Thanksgiving dinner, my friend and I started on our preplanned trip to Montreal. My friend had retired and planned to return to Moncton, his birthplace. He looked forward to being in daily contact with his siblings and relatives. His SUV was loaded with the last of his possessions. We drove through Detroit and through the bridge to Canada, and once on the 401, we stopped for the night. We awakened very early the next morning and proceeded with our plan to reach Montreal within eight hours. Winter in Canada can be brutal and treacherous, given the abundance of snow and icy roads. When we started out, it was snowing. The roads were slushy and icy, and visibility was poor. Driving through Canada's winter storms was something with which my friend was familiar, as he made frequent trips there years before I met him. Initially, I tried to relax so that I would not make him nervous. However, the semis on the road concerned me. I suggested that we find a motel, sleep, and in the morning resume our trip. He said he was alert, not sleepy, and anxious to get to Montreal. I did not press the issue.

It was November 29 and about 10:00 a.m. when I noted a huge semi next to us. Instinctively I held on to the armrests as the semi expelled a blanket of slush that covered the entire windshield. I feared that the semi was going to sideswipe the SUV. It did and crashed into the passenger side. In seconds, the SUV was out of control and slammed into a cement wall on the driver's side. The semi's driver did not stop. We were able to exit the van without help and before anyone appeared to assist us. The damage to the van was severe—the sides, back, and front were crushed. It did not take long for the police, a tow truck, and an ambulance to arrive on the scene. My friend and I did not appear to be hurt and refused the service of the ambulance. A lovely young lady going in the opposite direction stopped her car and walked across the highway to offer assistance. She escorted me to her car, where she kept the motor running to keep me warm. Who would believe that again we were stranded in Kingston on the 401? And this gracious young lady is an entertainer and on her way to an engagement. Yet she stopped to help us. One does not forget incidents and kindness such as hers.

The SUV was towed to Jack's Towing Service. Mr. Dennis Wilkinson, an account executive from Budget Car and Truck Rental, was at the towing office when we arrived. We proceeded to his office to discuss solutions to our problem. The gentleman was sympathetic and supportive as we discussed options to the dilemma in which we found ourselves. The major problem was finding a rental car that could be driven to Moncton, where it could be returned. The latter is not possible in Canada. In the end, with Dennis's help, we were able to rent a van that would meet our needs and drove it to his sister's home in Montreal. She was anticipating our visit because we had informed her of our accident as soon as a phone was available. A second call notified her that we would be arriving in Montreal in about five hours. We could not fit all of our belongings in the rented van. With the repair shop owner's approval, they would remain in the SUV in the towing yard until we were in a position to reclaim them. The kindness shown to us by the people of Kingston was encouraging and helped to reduce our anxiety, thereby maintaining focus on our predicament. We proceeded to Montreal.

It was with relief and joy that my friend's sister greeted us upon our arrival at her home. She had been worried and feeling helpless as there did not seem to be anything she could do to help with the situation in which we found ourselves. She was brought up to date on the details of our accident and aftermath. Anticipating our visit, she had prepared dinner after our second phone call to her, advising her that we were able to rent a van. We had given her the time to expect us. As we ate, we discussed the issues of how to return the rented van to Kingston and how to retrieve our belongings, which were in the SUV. Then the major question was how to reach our final destination—Moncton. After considerable mulling, one of us proposed trying to get one of their relatives to come to Montreal with a vehicle to, *first,* return the van to the rental agency; *second,* remove our belongings from the crippled van and place its contents into the relative's vehicle; *third,* return to Montreal; and *fourth,* reach our final destination—Moncton—with our belongings.

To make an involved story short, a young nephew living in St. Edward's Island offered to take time off from work to help his uncle. Two of my friend's male siblings, living in Moncton, were retired and agreed to accompany their nephew on the awesome task of completing the tasks above, beginning with driving the ten or more hours from Moncton to Montreal. To undertake this arduous mission from start to finish, the men took turns driving.

I was impressed by the way his relatives, without question, came to our aid. One of the benefits was that the Moncton relatives and Montreal sister, who do not see each other often, got to visit each other; and it enhanced and enlivened the arduous effort made to help us. The camaraderie between brothers, nephew, and sister and their humorous interaction lightened the burden.

After resting in Montreal for about two days, the brothers and nephew proceeded to complete the exhausting process of returning the rented vehicle to Kingston, retrieving my friend's belonging still in the SUV, and placing them in the nephew's van. When all tasks were completed, all four males took turns making the return to Moncton nonstop. Upon their arrival at Moncton, their relatives greeted the rescuers with relief and joy that the mission had been completed trouble free.

A few days after arriving in Moncton, I began to have headaches so severe that, intermittently, I held my head, hoping to ease the pain. Finally, I asked my friend if he would drive me to a masseuse from whom I had received massages when I visited Moncton. The masseuse worked on me for more than one hour, and by the time I left her office, my headache had subsided but left me with a dull pain. After spending about ten days in Moncton with my friend and his family, I flew home.

# 55

When I returned home, my life continued without the presence of my friend. I did miss him but adjusted to his absence. Headaches recurred from time to time. They were not severe and were relieved with Tylenol. I began to have difficulty walking, climbing stairs, and dancing. On August of 2003, the tests my personal doctor ordered showed I had elevated levels of inflammation. On two separate appointments with the doctor to whom she referred me, I was told that I might have arthritis, rheumatoid arthritis, or cancer, etc. I was stunned. At the two appointments with this doctor, she sat a distance away from me as she gave me this news and never did she approach me to examine my body. I was livid with her coldness and indifference. I reported her to my personal physician. She was appalled by the manner in which I was given the dire news of her medical conclusions. She was sympathetic and told me that she would take care of the issue personally. She made an appointment for me with another doctor.

It has been my daily practice to pray and meditate before starting the day's tasks. For years, I was involved with yoga and had monthly massages. Given my present physical condition, I was not remiss in maintaining these practices, and I added one more massage, making it two per month. The doctors who treated me could not pinpoint the source of my problem. The medical tools prescribed, such as MRIs and Dopler, did not identify the source of the problems I was having. Physical therapy did not help. I insisted to my doctors that the problem was related to my knees and followed that by holding my two knees. Then something peculiar happened about a year after receiving massages. At a treatment, for the first time, the masseuse applied an electrical probe to the area of my knees that I believed was responsible for the problems I was having. Two days after having had the probe treatment, I was awakened about two o'clock in the morning by a burning sensation between my legs from the groin to below my knees. The area was so hot that I could barely touch it. I live alone and would not indulge in panic. I made myself relax, prayed, and slowly the heat, which lasted for more than two hours, dissipated. And for the first time in over a year, I was able to get out of bed without sliding off of it.

At my next appointment two weeks later with the masseuse, I informed her about my experience with the heat I felt two days after my treatment. She expressed surprise, stating that none of her clients had ever reported this happening to them nor had she heard of anyone who had a similar experience after the use of the probe. She proceeded with the massage and again used the electrical probe. It may be unbelievable to some, but on the second day of the massage, I felt the same intense heat. And I was able now to walk upstairs but still had some difficulty walking downstairs. An MRI had been scheduled by one of my doctors for my torso and my knees. Lo and behold, two days after the MRI I felt the heat reported above with the probe, but it was not as intense. The MRI showed that I had torn cartilage on both knees. And to my relief, I was able to resume most normal activities, walk up and downstairs, and slow dance with caution. My mobility continued to improve. In hindsight, I believe that as the semi threw the vehicle from one side to the other, my knees slammed against each other.

I kept the scheduled appointment that my personal physician had made for me with an orthopedic physician. What a marked difference from the experience I had with the former specialist. This doctor used a probe (not electrical) on virtually every part of my body and concentrated on the knees. I related to him the experience with the intense heat I experienced from my groin to below my knees after having had two massages and an MRI, with the result that my mobility was almost normal. He had never heard of this happening to anyone that has been in his care. When he finished his examination, he reported that the examination of my knees showed remarkable improvement and that surgery, which initially had been contemplated, was not to be considered. He was curious as to what I had been doing that brought about the improvement. I advised him of my morning ritual that included meditation, yoga exercises, biweekly massages, and prayers. He advised me to keep on with the practices in which I was involved. As for an explanation for my experience with the heat between my thighs, I can only believe that it was a miracle answer to my prayers!

This physician was considerate, listened to my discouragement with the ineffective medical tools, and was gentle. I thanked my personal doctor for sending me to a physician who cared. I must give thanks to the insurance company for paying all medical and non medical costs involved and supporting me with the course I took in order to heal. It is my impression that what I had used to get well, in the end, was cheaper than the extensive surgery and physical therapy that would have been necessary. To this day, I walk straight and pain free, thanks first to God to whom I prayed for relief, the masseuse, the yoga, and the last MRI that replicated the incidents with the masseuse's use of the electrical probe. Thanks also to my personal doctor, who, after my complaint about the ineffectual physician, made an appointment for me with a doctor who cared.

I made one or two more trips to Canada to visit my friend. I believe we both realized that a distance between us was not conducive to maintaining a relationship. All I asked of him was that if he found someone in Moncton or its vicinity to let me know and I would understand. He did, and that was the end of a friendship that lasted more twenty years. I think back to the pleasant times we shared and have no regrets. I was blessed to have met his family and the close relationship I had with them even though I realized it was at an end.

# 56

Toward the end of October of 2003, I received a call from my Canadian friend's niece to let me know that her mother, Vickie, was seriously ill and her death was imminent. Vickie was my friend's brother's wife. His niece added that if I wished to see her mother, I should not delay. Vickie and I had developed a close friendship throughout the years, and I wanted very much to see her before her death. I immediately made arrangements to fly to Moncton, and upon arrival, I was met at the airport by Vickie's daughters. I stayed with Vickie's family throughout my visit.

The evening of my arrival, I accompanied her husband and her daughters to the hospital. Vickie's welcome at seeing me was worth the hassle of preparing for the unanticipated trip. With one or two members of her family, I was able to visit her, twice daily, for three days before she died. She held my hand throughout our visits. Whenever a hospital staff person came into her room, she looked up at them and, after introductions, said, "She came all the way from Chicago to see me." Her reception of me and the happiness she showed toward me whenever we visited warmed my heart. Her daughters, her husband, and I were with her on the day expected to be her last day. However, we left because her nurse suggested we return home since Vickie seemed to be fine. She did not expect death to be imminent. I felt uneasy as we left her room. Minutes after we returned home, the phone rang, and we were told to return to the hospital immediately because Vickie was dying. We arrived too late! I remained with her family throughout the funeral, the luncheon, and stayed on until the date of my departure, a few days after the funeral.

A few months later my friend called to inform me that his sister Yvonne died. She lived in Montreal. Although for several years she had been having medical problems, she continued to enjoy life. She enjoyed telling and laughing at jokes. She was a vibrant woman, and it was always a pleasure to be in her company. Several times, at her invitation, I visited her in Montreal. We communicated by phone often. She was a true friend, seldom judgmental, and we exchanged conversation easily. With Vickie and Yvonne's deaths, although a distance away from me, I lost two of my best friends, whom, to this day, I miss.

# 57

Throughout the many years since my mother's death, thoughts of her surfaced periodically. From time to time, I looked at the funeral photo, focusing on her and briefly on the baby. It had never occurred to me that the little person in that coffin was without an identity and with no indication that she, too, was in it. To my knowledge no one had thought about her, and in my presence, she was never mentioned. Yet looking at the photo, I was impressed at how nicely, and hopefully lovingly, someone had dressed her. It was during the month of August of 2001 that I had dreams where my mother was the focus. From time to time, I was plagued with my mother's death and how it may have affected me. I did not believe I could delve into this area without help. I contacted a professional, who had helped me in the past and had some knowledge of my life. I made appointments with her and, on the advice of a professional friend, with a respected hypnotherapist.

The sessions with the therapist were intense. In one of the sessions, after discussing my mother's death, I broke down sobbing. When the therapist softly asked what was going on, I replied that I may have seen my mother as she was dying. I described the scene I envisioned, adding that on at least one other occasion, this possibility had occurred to me. The therapist dealt with me with concern and not with disbelief. It is not necessary, and it would be painful for me to add further to the session with this therapist. The therapist's belief and caring was healing; and sixty-eight years after my mother's death, on October 9, 2001, I wrote a four-page letter from the heart to my mother, a letter inspired through meditation.

When I met with the hypnotherapist, I told him about my sessions with the therapist. He deviated from my mother's death and took a different path. The reader may not be aware that when one is under hypnosis, the patient generally is not always in control. The training and personal experience I had with hypnosis and the belief I had in the discipline made me an easy client. After relaxing me, he asked, "What do you wanted to work on?" I replied, "My Mexicanism." I added that when I brought up this subject with other therapists they had difficulty accepting that I had trouble with my ethnicity. He, too, stated that he was not prone to accept it as a major problem. Then he said that he would like to take another avenue and asked about my inner child—had I come to terms with her, am I able to hold her, accept her, and so forth. My response was that I had never thought about having an inner child. With that, as he spoke to me, "my subconscious took over," and focus was on my childhood after my mother's death. At one point I stated that perhaps what I needed to do was to accept the forlorn picture I had of this inner child.

Under hypnosis, the image I had of this inner child after her mother's death was not one I liked or one with whom I wished to be associated. Who would want to admit to being a child who was a bed wetter, who fainted without warning, vomited, was a picky eater, withdrawn, and scared? So focus was on getting in touch with this inner child, the label given by the hypnotist. Gently he encouraged me to recognize the strength and bravery she manifested to get me through the difficult period. After the session, the task assigned was to get in touch with my inner child, to make friends with her, hold her, and to write her a letter thanking her for getting me through the difficult period in my life. The letter was written on August 22, 2001. As a result, I no longer look upon my inner child as someone with whom I did not want to associate but one who was a vital part of my growth. She provided me with the strength to endure the downs in my life, leaving me to enjoy the ups, of which I enjoy many.

In retrospect, I cannot understand why the child prior to my mother's death, whose personality was totally different from the inner child described to the hypnotherapist, never came up in our sessions. I neglected telling my therapist and hypnotherapist that the inner child that he focused on was quite different from the child before my mother's death. I wonder why I buried her, ignored her in these sessions. These two children that I was had markedly different personalities. The first, as I recall, was outgoing; the second, withdrawn. A prior therapist did allude to a difference between the child prior to my mother's death and after. Once, she stated that from time to time she had seen a happy little girl peek out, especially when I revealed a sense of humor as we discussed serious issues. It is my belief that "the trip through my life" with the help of professionals has united the two and, both contributed to the person I am today. The issue does not concern me any longer. However, on March 2, 2001, early in the morning, thoughts of the inner child persisted, and a poem I wrote on April 19, 1967 entered my mind. I presume I wrote it after a therapy session, one to which to date I had paid little attention to. It seems appropriate at this point.

## Conflict

When all is done,
Three Persons are meshed in one,
All wanting to take a role,
All wanting to live in this soul.

Each had contributed its share,
Each had its trials to bear,
Each in its time has hungered for a place—
A feeling of belonging to the human race.

# 58

As mentioned earlier, unless there is an unforeseen interruption, before the day's tasks, I have made it a practice to begin the day reading the Bible, meditating, and exercising. Often, meditation has prepared me for happy or hurtful events with which I must deal. On occasion, unfinished or important issues may break through the meditation. The reader will recall that my mother died in childbirth, taking her infant child with her. A photo was taken of her and her infant in the casket, outside St. Benedict's Catholic Church, at which her life was celebrated. It clearly shows the infant positioned at the left side of her mother's head. This point is being made because after her death, no one in the family or relatives, to my knowledge, ever mentioned this little being. Further, the cemetery marker bears only our mother's name. The appointments with the therapist and hypnotherapist may have been the impetus behind the content of my mediation in August of 2001.

One morning, as I was deep in meditation, I was brought out of it by my sobbing. I was frightened by the appearance of a vision—a lady dressed in white, looking down at me. Immediately I thought of my mother. With that I focused on her coffin, in which there laid another body, the body of the tiny girl who had never been neither acknowledged nor named on the marker. There was no outward indication that she even existed! I sobbed unceasingly, and I could not rid myself of my mother's death and her unborn child. Perhaps I was crying for my baby sister, whom I never knew. Through my sobbing, the thought came to me that my mother was giving me a message—to do something about my nameless sister. With that I calmed down and made a decision to correct this omission. First, I had to contact my three sisters, from the oldest to the youngest, Trini, Mary, Marge. I have been closer to Mary. I contacted her and asked her to call our other sisters and tell them that I needed to see them about an important matter and set the following Sunday to met with them.

Naively, I believed that taking care of the aforementioned issue would put an end to my persistent thoughts about our mother and that my sisters would support what I was called to do. To say I was surprised by their response, when I presented to them the importance of adding our sister's name to our mother's marker, is an understatement. My oldest sister, Trini, vehemently avowed that there was no baby in the coffin and persisted in her denial. I asked her to look at the photo taken outside the church. As for my younger sister, I can be more understanding of the disinterest she showed when I brought up the subject.

In the interests of preserving my younger sister's privacy, the following events are condensed. Marge, beginning at age two, experienced the same unexplained, rapid changes in her life that I did. One can only imagine what a toddler experiences at the loss of her mother and the abandonment by her sister, her caretaker, whose whereabouts were unknown. Then, at age five, she spent time in Kansas City to be cared for by aunt Silveria. According to Mary Bustamante, aunt Silveria's daughter, because she seemed to be unhappy, cried and apparently missed her family; she was returned to her home to be with her family. At that time, Trini was our caretaker. Unexpectedly, seven years after our mother's death, our father, unbeknownst to his children, remarries. Trini and our stepmother were constantly at odds. Apparently, because our father believed he had no other option, he separated the family. He provided a separate camp unit for him and his wife while his children remained in the original unit. Soon disaster hits the family again. Unbeknown to anyone and without due regard for her family, in broad daylight, Trini eloped with the brother of our sister Joan's husband—whereabouts unknown. Our father reunited his family. The final separation from the family, I believe, was when my sister attended a Catholic high school in Chicago. The school had a facility similar to that of a boarding school, and it was her home for her four years of high school. To my recollection, she was allowed home visits and visitations. I believe summers were spent with our family. Many changes were occurring in her family, and no one considered their effect on this young person. Many adults, including my father, failed to or do not believe it necessary to inform their young children when changes are occurring in their home and give little consideration to the effect they have on them. Many years later, in January of 1975, Marge's youngest son, Steven Orozco, died unexpectedly as a result of an aneurysm. He had just turned thirteen.

Based on what she endured as a young child, I can understand why my sister removed herself from the issue of having our sister's name on the marker. My sister Mary was more accepting of what needed to be done. There was a discussion as to what name would be used, and

I asked our sister Trini whether she had heard our parents talking about what name to give the coming addition to the family. She stated that the only name she remembered was "Concepcion." There was consensus that this was the name to be used on the marker.

# 59

On August 24, 2001, after ending my daily meditation, I called my sister Mary and asked her if she heard from our other two sisters about having the name for our mother's child etched on the marker. I was taken aback by what she reported. In sum, Mary reported that they (our sisters) could not understand why this was coming up so many years later. They questioned why this could not have been done shortly or a few years after their deaths. My sisters gave no thought to the shock my father, older siblings, and relatives suffered by our mother's sudden and unexpected death. In the preparations and upheaval the baby had unintentionally been ignored insofar as the marker was concerned. It is likely that no one ever had to deal with an issue such as this. Possibly they did not think of this stillborn infant as a person. My sisters said that they could not feel or think as I was thinking because it was something I was going through and not they. Mary added that if I wanted to proceed with my plan it was okay with her and that probably it would be okay with our sisters, but they would not take an active part in this undertaking. As she related the foregoing to me, I felt alone with my wish to right a grave omission. It was not easy for me to note this callousness from my sisters. I had asked Mary to help by checking with St. Benedict's Church to find out if there was a baptismal certificate for the child. She reported there was none. With a good-bye, we hung up.

Understandably, I was quite hurt by my sisters' indifference, but I also realize that they may not as yet have come to terms with our mother's death as I am doing now. I had a strong need to connect with my inner child so that I would not be alone as I brought closure to our mother's and sister's deaths—at least for my relief. From their responses above, I realized that whatever the cost, I could not count on them for help. After I obtained the death certificates for Ildefonda (correct spelling, Ildefonsa) Lopez and the certificate of stillbirth for Baby Girl Lopez, I made a visit to St. Benedict's Cemetery. I was given a copy of burial arrangements showing the interment date of November 22, 1932, the day of Cecelia's birthday, our oldest sister. The caretaker informed me that the cemetery had nothing to do with markers. I was given a list of five granite/memorial companies located near Blue Island. I selected the most likely company and personally made a trip there and informed them of my need. I was told that if the name could be added to the present marker, the cost would be considerably lower. However, if it became necessary to replace old the marker because of limited space to include on the baby's name, the cost would be considerably higher. Fortunately, there was ample room on the old marker and the name "Concepcion" could be inscribed on it.

I had given my sisters the information the granite caretaker had given me—that the cost of the inscription depended on whether the name could be inscribed on the old marker or whether the marker had to be replaced. They were unresponsive. Neither was there a comment made nor was there an offer to help defray its cost. I was too proud to ask for it, and I could not endure the rejection if I were refused. In the end, I was relieved to learn that there was enough room on the marker for Concepcion's name. I thanked God that I was able to bear the cost without their help, and if the marker had to be replaced, I was not about to lower myself to ask for their help. I made out a check to the granite company. No one informed me to let me know when the work was completed. I did learn via the grapevine that my sister's name had been added to the marker. Then it occurred to me that the marker should be blessed. I asked my sister Mary if she could contact one of the priests at St. Benedict's Church and ask whether he was available for this task. She was a member of the church and maintained a good relationship with the priests. She said she would. Periodically I asked if she had a positive answer from them. Each time she would tell me that they were willing to do so whenever they had time.

# 60

And so time marched on and I was busy with other matters. So to my chagrin, it was not until 2010 that I finally gave up on waiting for help from my sister on the blessing of the marker. Furthermore, my sister Mary was grieving over her husband, who died on November 17, 2009. One of my nephews, John Rangel, had been ordained a deacon. It occurred to me that perhaps it was within the purview of his deaconship to bless the marker. I contacted him and explained that I had succeeded in having the unborn baby's name engraved on his grandmother's marker and now wanted it to be blessed. He agreed to undertake the task and the date of May 21, 2010 between 9:00 a.m. and 10:00 a.m. was set. When I called to inform my younger sister, Marge, of the date for the blessing, she replied that she would have to check with her children to find out what plans they had. I told her that I realized it was her birthday and that setting the date was not intentional, that it was the date that accommodated the deacon's schedule. I did not hear from her. As it turned out, my nephew had to change the date because of conflict with a commitment for his church, and it took precedence. He suggested changing the day to Memorial Day at 9:00 a.m. because on that day, he had to be in attendance for the Mass at the cemetery.

So on the following Sunday, Memorial Day, the deacon, his wife, Anne, and a niece, Agnes Espinoza, were with me to complete the task I had undertaken. Never did any of my sisters mention the blessing of the marker.

On October 22, 1966, I wrote the following poem after a therapy session, which seems appropriate at this time.

### Bittersweet

The past is laid to rest,
Forever to remain at peace.
Painful memories will no more test
This mortal's strength, oh bittersweet release.

Gone are the shackles of yesteryear,
That held me in bondage and fear.

There remains but a bearable ache,
The residue of a wound that kept burning,
By a yearning whose hold I could not break,
Without the help of someone's patience and learning

As stated above, the delay in completing the blessing of the marker was due to my being busy with other matters, in particular the trip to Canada in 2002, the accident before we reached our destination, and a subsequent visit in 2003. Being busy with other events in my life should not have been the reason for my neglect.

# 61

To continue with events in my life, I must go back to the mid-1970s, when I was a student in the University of Illinois, Chicago Circle Campus's Psychology Department (UICC). I had developed an interest in how social service agencies monitored or evaluated their programs. I approached a United Way Agency near my home, explained to the executive director that I was a student at the aforementioned university, and that I was interested in developing a model for evaluating social-service programs. It would be classified as an independent study for credit. The director was interested in my plan and graciously gave me space in their office. Also, a typewriter was available for my use. Soon thereafter, I was invited by one of the supervisors of one of its programs to accompany him to an early morning (6:00 a.m.) informal meeting at a local restaurant with businessmen, professionals, self-employed males, and others for coffee. Every weekday morning, without fail, there were at least ten men in attendance. A few of them I knew personally or by their status in the community. Except on rare occasion, I was the only female present. On rare occasions, a few wives of the attendees joined the gathering. I was accepted as a member of the group. It was an enjoyable way to begin the morning, Monday through Friday and

I looked forward to the camaraderie, the bantering, and exchange of ideas.

One morning, a man, unknown to anyone in the group, came into the restaurant, approached the group, and introduced himself as John Reed. He was invited to join us. The man was handsome, polite, neatly dressed, and joined in the ongoing conversations easily. He informed the group that he was a newcomer to the area. He had an impressive background with some of the largest investment companies and had decided to go into business for himself. His office was located less than two blocks from the restaurant. He was divorced and the father of two daughters. In a short time, this man became aware of all the members' businesses and that I was a school psychologist. In hindsight, I surmise that he may have obtained background information on some of the members of the group soon after joining it.

A few days later, he asked me about the type of investments I had. I mentioned an IRA and some stocks with well-known companies. He asked if I would be interested in meeting him at his office to go over my portfolio. He stated that he might be able to do better than what I was currently getting from my investments. Within the week, I met with him. He looked over my IRA account, and he pointed out that over the years I had it, growth was negligible. I turned it over to him, and he put it in a Venture program. Subsequently, in January of 1998, he transferred it to Jackson National Life, because Venture was not meeting his expectations. Shortly thereafter, he sold me two annuities with Jackson National Life. At that time, I was not aware that some experts in the field did not consider annuities to be the best investment if one wanted to reap the maximum benefits from one's money. Because I had limited knowledge about investments, I let the matter rest. On the plus side, my investments with him were showing a remarkable increase in value. And he was learning a great deal about me and my life.

I cannot remember whether John Reed informed me that he was closing his office in Highland and taking a position with Chase Manhattan Mortgage Company. I do not believe that he did. Now communication I received from him regarding my investments was under a Chase letterhead. Further, phone communication between us was with the Chase office in Schererville, Indiana. From this point, I am confused and unsure of the sequence of events. In the spring of 2005, I liquidated my IRA with Jackson National Life and signed it over to J. C. Reed & Company while, it appeared, he was still in the employ of Chase Manhattan, the office located in Orland Park, Illinois. Somewhat later, he informed me about his move to Franklin, Tennessee, and starting his own mortgage company, namely, J. C. Reed & Company. Then through a form letter, I learned that he transferred my IRA to PENSCO Trust Company. Periodically he kept in touch with me via phone and visited me when he came to Munster, Indiana, to visit his daughters.

From here on in, my relationship with the Reed Company gets complicated. I must admit that he presented an excellent visual profile of his new company. All of his propaganda was presented in a costly and elaborate fashion. It was impressive. In starting his own company, Reed hoped to fulfill his dream of working in rural Tennessee and Kentucky to educate its semiliterate population on how to use the banking system to improve their lives. He believed that they had little knowledge of banks and how to benefit from the services provided—mainly savings and checking accounts. He wished to make them knowledgeable in how to buy and own their own homes and so forth.

I have always been prudent with my funds and hesitated to enter into something about which I knew nothing. I presented his propaganda to a few relatives and friends, who admitted they knew nothing about the type of business he was getting into. It was not without hesitancy that I agreed to invest in his newly established company. Foolishly I believed that because of the monies I had accumulated with Jackson National Life, I owed him and was seduced by his desire to improve the lives of the people living in Tennessee and Kentucky. I did not give thought to the fact that he had already made handsome commissions from my Jackson holdings.

In March and September of 2005, my two annuities with Jackson National Life were surrendered to J. C. Reed Mortgage Bankers, both totaling over $33,000. He already had control of my IRA. On the annuities and IRA, early withdrawal losses were substantial. This concerned me and I called him about the losses. He assured me that I would make up the losses in a short time. He was very persuasive and smooth, and in August, 2005, I made out a check for $15,500 and, in September, one for $15,000.00 to J. C. Reed & Co.

In 2006, Reed visited me, and after informing me of the continued progress being made by his company, he told me that he had been diagnosed with colorectal cancer. I was flabbergasted and speechless to believe that this young man, a former marine, as fit and healthy as his appearance suggested, could be struck with such a serious illness. I expressed my deep sorrow at his news. Earlier that year, he had brought his fiancée to my home so that I could meet her. On March 3, 2007 he wrote me a business letter addressed to me personally, expressing his appreciation for my friendship, love, and support over the years. In addition, his report of his company's progress was positive and glowing. On a PS at the end of the letter, he wrote a personal note on his health. I am omitting the first sentence because it was what followed that moved me—"God has a plan, and I am okay with not knowing the details of that plan. My family and I are in very good hands. Thanks so much for your prayers and friendship!"

A friend, whom I had introduced to John Reed and had invested in his company, and I visited Reed in the hospital in 2006 after his intensive invasive surgery. He had several surgeries after that. He died on June 7, 2008. Imagine my shock when on November 18, 2008, SEC closed his office for fraudulent practices. Further shock was finding out that shortly before the closing, SEC had begun its investigation into the company in June! I reviewed and totaled the amount I had invested in his company and compared it to what his company recorded. I found that it was $15,000 short. I recalled that I had given him two separate checks, one for $15,000 in August and one for $15,500 in September. I obtained copies of the front and back of the checks and found that one of the checks ($15,500) had been endorsed with the company stamp and the other with, I presume, John C. Reed's signature. Looking closely at the somewhat-blurred endorsements, it is not easy to identify the date the checks were cashed. One can note that they were not cashed in Franklin, nearby Nashville, or any other Tennessee towns but in Kentucky, at one of the company's Franklin/Nashville bank's branches. Both amounts were noted in his first rough financial report to his investors dated November 20, 2005. Believing in his integrity, I had not suspected underhanded investment practices and did not periodically total up and review my figures with his company's investment reports. It was too late to address the omission.

All of the company's employees, who had direct contact with Reed's clients, were impeccably dressed, well mannered, handsome, and suave—in short, one might say, replicas of Reed's persona. His office personnel, too, were well trained and very personable. All employees knew exactly the information that was to be given to the stockholders. I made frequent calls concerning my holdings and was assured that the company was doing exceedingly well, beyond expectation, and hiring people to meet the demand. My investment monies had been placed in two pockets. One held my IRA, and the other monies were placed in a trust account. In reviewing my records, it appears that during the first quarter of 2006, an alliance was made with a well-known established investment firm. From that time, investment results were issued from that company under its logo, below which an extensive investment report was rendered. I was doing so well that my friends questioned what I was doing. Unfortunately, to their misfortune, I referred them to Reed's company; and they invested their savings with Reed. My friends were thrilled and amazed by the glowing reports received each month. Also, the company had moved to new and larger quarters that were being "tailored to meet its growing needs."

The growth of the company, noted on financial reports, was beyond belief; and it should have raised a red flag. My years of friendship with President Reed and his work experience in the area of investment obscured any thought that he was capable of wrongdoing. I was blinded and in denial that he was culpable in the fiasco of his "dream." In providing the inflated glowing—now apparently falsified— reports sent to the stockholders, he is culpable in manipulating the expectations and feelings of his predominantly elderly clientele. He made a mockery of the elderly, who deserved better treatment. After my daughter and I visited the new "office," notable by the *absence of any employees,* I now question whether his growing needs were of a personal nature—food for his perhaps shaky ego.

# 62

Although I desperately wanted to attend John's funeral, it was not feasible at that time for me to get away. A week later, I asked my daughter Marcie if she would help me drive to Franklin, Tennessee, to visit his grave. We stopped at the newly built office building to get directions to cemetery.

The barrenness of the office should have raised questions in my mind. The absence of staff was puzzling, but in view of John's recent death, I did not want to think that anything was amiss. There was only one person attending the office. I asked the female attendant if we could view the section of the building that would house the most up-to-date office equipment available, deemed necessary to expand the company's program. We were taken through the beautiful, well-equipped, *empty* offices; and then we came to an area that had a security keypad requiring a code. As we looked through the glass-enclosed area, the layout and the business equipment were impressive. The absence of anyone at work in the whole building and in this section, however, was puzzling. I did not question it. The clerk used the code on the security keypad to let us into this area. She informed us that because this section held important information, no one, other than the few employees who would be using the equipment and designated management, had access to the code for the keypad for admission into the section. The red flags should have been flying, but I continued to be blinded by my faith and trust in my friend. I noted above that SEC was already investigating the company. On the day my daughter and I visited the new office, we did not see anyone other than the female who escorted us through the building. On the way home, my daughter questioned the total absence of employees, stating that it was not normal. I said nothing.

With the directions provided by the one staff member present, we located the cemetery. There were three freshly dug graves. We were unable to pinpoint the one in which my friend was interred. The markers had not been erected. After we left the cemetery, we went shopping, to lunch, and then home. I was disappointed at not locating his grave. On the way home I was subdued and puzzled at finding the absence of workers and lack of activity in the new office.

On November 18, 2008, five months after his death, the SEC closed Reed's company due to fraudulent practices. The closure of the company was a travesty for all who bought into his "dream" of helping the semiliterate people of Tennessee and Kentucky. I do not wish to bore the reader with details. Anyone interested in the fraud can log on to SEC, Case 3:08-cv-01112, document 1, filed on November 18, 2008 (J. C. Reed & Co.). Many of the investors lost the major portion of their life's savings. And I was riddled with guilt because of the losses incurred by my friends, most of whom were elderly.

This man's despicable scheme was an outright theft of the dream of the elderly, whom he fleeced, to enjoy a retirement free of financial stress. As for me, more important than the loss of my monetary assets was the probability that I would lose friends I held in high esteem and valued. It has not been easy for me to come to terms with the betrayal I felt from someone I trusted and, yes, loved. He was like a son to me. It has not been easy for me to cast aspersions on the man whom I held in high regard—one who was my friend for more than twenty years. Some of my friends of many years were understandably hurt; it seemed to them that I was disregarding their loss because of my inability, initially, to accept that he sought to enrich his life and financial status at their expense. That they were hurt because I seemed to put him first is understandable. It was not my intent to dismiss their pain and suffering—caused by the collapse of his empire—by my seeming support. I was torn between the two. There should have been no question as to who merited my allegiance!

# 63

In February of 2009, my friends and I, along with many of the other investors, engaged the services of a law firm who undertook to represent us in a class-action lawsuit. We were made aware that it was not possible we would recoup the total amount of our losses. It is my belief that most of us would have been grateful to recoup a reasonable portion of our loss. We anxiously awaited the outcome of the suit. In December of 2010, we were informed by the law firm that a settlement had been reached, and soon, we received a partial return of our investment. Many were disappointed that it was not as generous as we hoped. I was chagrined by the return I was granted. It was about half of what was expected because of the manner in which the company sold my IRA to another company for an amount less than its original value.

The following is one example of how my IRA funds were *recycled* to provide funds so that the company could continue *expanding* and *spending* without detection by many of the unsuspecting and trusting clients. As mentioned earlier, my monies were placed in two separate pockets, IRA and trust accounts. The latter held monies from annuities, stock holdings that were surrendered to the company, and cash. The IRA required that I withdraw the maximum amount prescribed by law from it. I asked that my withdrawal be sent to me quarterly and specified the amount I wished withdrawn. The withdrawal was always lower than that prescribed by the IRS. That was a huge mistake!

Because I was concerned that I might have trouble with the IRS, I called the office to find out whether I would be in violation of the law if I did not withdraw the maximum amount. I was assured by the vice president that the government did not care what I did with the money. As long as I took it out, I could do with it as I pleased. The company placed put the excess of the mandated withdrawal in my trust account with the intent, I believe, of having my money at their disposal to use as their need arose. The company was recycling my money! When I reviewed the glowing investment reports and the remarkable growth shown on both accounts, their practice did not concern me, and I considered it to be for my benefit. "A fool and his money are soon parted" is applicable to me! Had I taken the maximum amount out of my IRA, it would not have gone into my trust account and available for the company's benefit.

Losing my retirement monies was a serious loss, but the betrayal by a "friend" I trusted, I felt more deeply. I have had difficulty dealing with the blame I feel for the losses my friends incurred through my introduction to this company. I trusted this man implicitly, and it angers me more that my friends took a tremendous hit by the depletion of their retirement nest egg. It will mean sacrificing luxuries to which they had looked forward in order to pay for emergencies that are bound to arise. My friends were robbed of experiencing the quality of life for which they had planned and saved. In time, I may be able to forgive my "friend" for my loss, but at the present time, I am having trouble giving him any leeway for the loss my friends incurred and for putting my friendships in jeopardy.

# 64

Prior to the loss I incurred by investing in my friend's "dream," I had one misfortune that preceded it and two that followed it. In September of 2008, just prior to the closing of the aforementioned company, I had a car accident in Hammond, Indiana. I was exiting the parking lot of one of the city's park department centers. As I turned the corner into the east-west road, I did not immediately see a city pickup truck that was driving west on the road into which I was turning. The driver's side of my car hit the passenger door of the pickup truck. Fortunately no one was seated in the passenger seat. The front left side of my car was crushed, and although the front fender and lights were dangling, I was able to drive it to the auto repair facility I patronized. The only damage on the city vehicle that I noted was the door. The damage reported to the insurance company was considerably more. Rightly, I was found to be responsible for the accident. However, I make note that the three lanes on this service road, with a turn lane in the middle, are very narrow.

Four months after the company's failure, in March of 2009, I had a second accident early in the morning, again in Hammond. It was 6:00 a.m., dark, and visibility was poor. I was on my way to help my two young grandsons get ready for school. I was driving north on the two-lane road on which there was a huge Dumpster parked on the lane I was driving, taking more than half of the lane. I saw a car coming south, and to make room for the car, I overcorrected, moved to the right, and hit the corner of the Dumpster, causing severe damage to the front and driver's side of my car. It was not drivable. There was no damage to the Dumpster. Although the collision was very loud, the driver driving south did not stop. A woman across the street came out with a phone in her hand and called the police. A man came out of a house in front of the Dumpster. It appeared that he was the owner, but when questioned by the police, he said he did not have the ownership papers. He said he would go for them. He left us and was gone about ten to fifteen minutes. When he returned he told the policeman that he did not have the ownership papers because the Dumpster belonged to someone living in Chicago. The insurance company took note that it was not my fault because the Dumpster was illegally parked. To my knowledge, a citation was not issued. After several futile attempts to contact the owner of the Dumpster, who listed an address in Chicago, the insurance company may have dropped the matter. I was not informed as to the outcome of this accident, but my insurance rates increased for the following year.

Two months later, on the day after Mother's Day, May 7, 2009, after having my car serviced at an Indianapolis Boulevard facility (Route 41), I decided to stop for milk at the department store located on the same street. It was about 10:00 a.m. Although the store was less than five blocks from my home, I seldom patronized it. I parked my car in the store's front lot—the only parking lot at that time—and entered the store. I was standing at the front of the store by the bread department, looking over the assortment of breads. Soon a young male—neatly dressed in a white shirt, black pants, and with nicely groomed black hair—approached me and, in Spanish, asked if I spoke the language. I answered in the affirmative. He proceeded to tell me that he was not from the area and was having difficulty locating a church and a lawyer with whom he had an appointment. He added that he needed help with a problem he had. He gave me the names of the church and lawyer. I told him that to my knowledge there was no such church nearby and that I did not recognize the name of the lawyer.

This man's demeanor and tone suggested he was nervous and desperate. He showed me a wad of bills that he stated amounted to $4000, the amount required to pay the lawyer for the service to be provided for him. I gave the wad little attention because I have known that some people will roll many one dollar bills and cover them with a few larger bills to impress others. I told him I was sorry that he was having difficulty but that I did not have the time to help him. I informed him that had to care for my grandchildren. He persisted in his plea for help. He reiterated that if he did not get help, he would lose a great deal of money. He turned a deaf ear to my response that I did not have time to help him. Then he pointed to a woman standing by the bread display about eight feet to my left and stated that she looked Spanish. She, too, was neatly dressed in a dark skirt, white blouse, and beige sweater. My guess was that she was in her forties. She had sunglasses placed above her forehead at her hairline. He asked if I would approach her and ask her if she spoke Spanish and, if she did, to ask her if she would help him. The woman did speak Spanish, and she expressed her willingness to help the man. Both of us returned to where the male stood. Never did I suspect that she might be his accomplice!

The man was very convincing as he explained his problem to the woman. And as he restated his dilemma, her facial expression suggested that she was sympathetic. She, too, told him that she had no knowledge of the person or church he sought. She turned to me and said maybe both of us would be able to help. I insisted that I did not have the time to help, but it fell on deaf ears. She stated we should go to her car, which by design, I now believe, was not parked in the store's lot but on the south end of the store. It had no markings for parking and was barren. I cannot understand or explain why I continued in their company. As if in a sleepwalking mode, and walking between them, I followed them across the store to the south exit and to her car. He added to his story that he had this lottery ticket that had been a winner in a recent drawing and that it had to be redeemed in Chicago. I am not knowledgeable about the lottery or how the business is run. He tried to entice us by promising to reward us with $20,000 each if we would help him. I told him I was not interested in the money and still insisted that I did not have the time to assist him in his plight.

Was I still in shock and numb from the recent loss of my savings through a fraudulent company and the two recent car accidents that account for my passivity in accompanying both of them to the woman's white van? Then without resistance, I allowed the woman to help me into the front passenger seat while he got into the backseat behind me. She went to the driver's seat and sat down. This man proceeded to tell us that he needed two persons who could come up with $20,000 each and to accompany him to Chicago to collect his winnings. Although I thought the latter was strange, I said nothing. The woman took the lottery ticket from the man, pulled out her cell phone, and showed me the phone number on the back of it and dialed it. The conversation with the agent on the phone was in English. She was told that, indeed, the ticket was a winner. Then she handed the phone to me so that the man on the phone could reiterate to me that the man who wanted our help was telling the truth. I realize today, and too late, that this was a bogus setup. I was told repeatedly to not tell anyone about the man's problem, especially about the lottery ticket. Except for the phone conversation with the bogus lottery agent, Spanish was used throughout this ordeal.

I have asked myself numerous times since this farce how I could have let myself be taken in by these two conniving, unscrupulous people. These two were slick! I found myself giving them information about the institutions with whom I did my banking and that my bank was not far. "Stupid is as stupid does" is something I remember someone said, and I was stupid. The woman stated that she lived nearby and pointed to a new development to the west and south of the store. She stated that she had $20,000 at home but that she had to be careful because her husband was at home sleeping, and he might wake up. She was afraid that he would ask why she wanted the money. She added that the money represented her father's savings, which were withdrawn so that he could qualify for disability.

The woman left us to go to her house to get the money. I was left in the car with the man. We conversed as if we were longtime friends. When I asked his name, he said it was Tomas (Thomas). Then I asked if he was illegal. He responded that he was. I reasoned that that was why he needed someone who spoke English to go with him to get his winnings. In a few minutes, the woman returned with an envelope under her arm. The smart person that, at this point, I was not would have asked to see the money. It did not occur to me! It did occur to me to ask for her name, to which she replied, "Guadalupe Martinez." Both were quick to provide their names, and both were fictitious.

The reader may wonder about the naiveté of the writer, given her educational and professional background. She is not and never has been streetwise. To add to my stupidity, I had revealed to them that I had $2,000 in cash in my home. Because I needed to use the bathroom and my home was nearby, I told them that we could stop there and I would get the money. Then we could go to my bank. When we arrived at my home, as I got out of the car, she, too, quickly got out and followed me into the house. I noted that the man started to get out of the car, and in a loud voice I said, "You are not coming into my home." He stayed in the van. As I proceeded to the master bedroom to use the bathroom, the woman scanned everything in sight. I stopped her and said, "You cannot come into my room." She stopped but continued her investigation of my house and its contents. When we left the house, as I was about to get into the car, she reminded me that I did not have the $2,000. I said, "Oh," and returned to the house for the money. At this point the reader may think this is unbelievable, but hang on, it gets worse.

The three of us proceeded to my bank, and instead of turning into the bank parking lot, she turned into a Wendy's restaurant parking lot. It is located directly across from the east side of the bank. I questioned this move, and quickly, the man said that he was very thirsty and needed a drink. The woman said it would be better since she and I could cross the street easily, adding that by the time we were done, he would have obtained his drink. I was very nervous at this point and was becoming suspicious (would the reader believe this!!). She and I crossed the street, entered the bank, and the account representative, who generally attended to my needs, looked at me and smiled.

The woman started to follow me to the account representative's desk, but I stopped her, saying, "You stay here. You cannot come to the desk with me." She stopped and remained in the waiting area. I proceeded to the representative's desk and, as I held her hand, told her what I wanted. Still holding her hand, I looked directly into her eyes, perhaps hoping that she would get a message that my behavior was strange. I told her to get into my account because I wanted to withdraw money from my checking and savings accounts and needed it in cash. She went into my account, and checking the balances, I told her that I wanted $5,000 from my checking account and $4,000 from my savings account. I left only several hundred dollars in each account. Why did I withdraw that much cash? They had no way of knowing how much I kept in these accounts. I continued holding her hand, still in the hope that the she would read the pleading in my eyes and note that something was amiss as I said, "Don't ask any questions. Don't ask me anything. I can't say anything." I parroted their mandate! The attendant left to go to the vault. When she returned, she handed me $9,000 in cash in a folder. I returned to the waiting area, and the woman and I exited the bank.

As we walked across the street to return to the van parked in the Wendy's lot, the envelope with the money was under my left arm. She grabbed me by the right arm and, holding me back, said, "You walk too fast." When we reached the van, the man said that he had a severe headache and needed relief. True to my helpful self, I replied that there was a Walgreen's at the corner of Ridge Road and Indianapolis. I fell right into their hands. When we arrived at the drugstore, the woman suggested she and I go into the store. Then while she looked for water to take the headache relief tablet, I could look for the medication. It took a while for me to locate the aisle where such material is shelved. When I got to the checkout station with the meds in hand, I asked the clerk if a woman had approached her with a water bottle. When she answered that no one had been at the cash register, I turned and ran out the door.

I cannot say that I was surprised that the van was not there. Quickly, I ran back into the store, and when I told the cashier what I feared, she called for the manager. The police appeared shortly after the manager's call. I answered all their questions and was asked to describe the criminals. The police asked me if there was anyone available to come to assist me. My son Mark was called, and when he arrived, he was shocked that I had let myself be duped in this fashion. In the meantime, the store manager had picked up images of the culprits on the store's video apparatus. The images of the thieves appeared as I had described them. The police continued their questioning with my son. When they learned my age, they then believed that I was an elderly woman, who was easy to deceive—until my son gave them a rundown of my educational and professional background.

# 65

Because the culprits knew where I lived, a squad car was sent to my home. It remained there for several hours in the event that these culprits returned, perhaps to break in and ransack it. My car was still at the Indianapolis store, and the problem was how to get it back to me. Solution: in separate cars, a policeman and my son, with me in his vehicle, drove to my home, where my son left his car. Then the policeman drove my son to the store to retrieve my car, and the officer was free to finish what still needed to be done on the case. My son drove my car to my home, stayed with me for a while, subsequently returning to his home in his vehicle. I went to my computer and wrote a five-page account of what I had been through during the two hours I was in the company of the criminals.

The next day, my daughter Judy accompanied me to the police station. The officer, to whom the case was assigned, conversed with us for more than two hours. As I went over the sequence of events and he learned about my education and the types of positions I had held through the years—mostly in the "helping" areas—his response made me feel better about what had happened. He stated that now he had a clearer understanding of how I had been manipulated by people who are skilled at deceiving unsuspecting individuals, especially preying on the elderly. I gave him a copy of the report I had written, and my daughter and I left to return home.

I have no definitive explanation as to what prompted me to continue in the company of these two perpetrators. Several times I had reiterated that I did not have the time to assist them further nor to accompany them to Chicago to collect his winnings. Further, I was not interested in his reward. This fell on deaf ears. The two had a mission, and that was to get as much from me as they could. The names they gave me, Tomas (no last name) and Guadalupe Martinez, without a doubt, were factitious names.

After the fact, I realized that the two had scouted the area and knew it well, and what they did not know, I filled in the gaps. Unsuspectingly I abetted them in their scam. I can give no explanation, except that I began to fear what they might do to me if I did not comply with their requests. It was a case of two against one. At the bank, I had hoped that the account representative would get the message I was sending—that is, continuously holding her hand as I presented my request. As I looked into her eyes, I hoped that she would look into my eyes, note my overall demeanor, and note that I was scared. Later she told me that as I sat at her desk, my back to the waiting area, the woman who had accompanied me into the bank paced back and forth. I did fear that these two scoundrels were aware of where I lived and were capable of harming me. Because my children were concerned for my safety, my son-in-law Steve and daughter Marcie arranged to have a security system installed in my home.

# 66

Why I did not stop the two scam artists at the times when I may have had the opportunity, I have no explanation. Toward the end, I was scared, especially when she grabbed my arm because I was walking too fast. Was I still in shock after the Reed loss? Perhaps! It had been and is difficult still to cope with the betrayal of a trusted friend, and I went about mechanically. It has bothered me to think that he may have used his faith to espouse honesty, thereby was able to lure unsuspecting elderly clients to buy into his mission. I truly hope I am wrong in this possibility. He may have fooled me but not the God in whom he professed to believe.

Not wanting to worry my children, I kept control of how devastated I was about the Reed loss. I do not recall that I cried. This latter loss could have been more serious because I was, physically, in the hands of professional criminals. I never cried but was scared and unsure as to how I would manage to be financially independent for the rest of my life. I had worked years after retirement and was careful with my earnings so that I would not be a financial burden or worry for my children. I can only offer the reader that while in the company of these two perpetrators, I may have been in a daze and obeyed in robot like fashion. I have determined that henceforth, I would not be too quick to help someone who asked for help, especially a stranger or one who asks me if I speak Spanish and, perhaps I should add, a "friend." In defense of my actions, I will say that I may be riddled with an excessive amount of trust and helping behavior, engrained in me by noting the behavior of my father, my uncles, relatives, my faith, and employment history. I thank God that I was unscathed by these con artists.

In addition to my mishaps, the years between 2000 and 2010 brought sorrow to many family members. Boniface Lopez, uncle Benito's son, died December 5, 2001. Trini Zavala, a sister, died on August 16, 2005. Phillip Rangel, nephew, was killed instantly on November 4, 2009. He was standing on a curb and was struck by an automobile. Uncle Benito lost two grandsons: Edward Valadez died on December 9, 2009, and his brother, Richard Valadez, died on May 9, 2010. And Anthony Lopez, my father's youngest son from his second marriage, died on June 7, 2010. He was diabetic, and both of his feet were amputated.

# 67

Plato, many years ago, reported that Socrates espoused the belief that an unexamined life is a life not worth living. This is a refrain that impressed me at an early age and took to heart. It may be the impetus for undertaking this journey through time to understand what made Erminia, a.k.a. Minnie, Lopez Rincon tick. For many years I have been compulsive about meditating and recording happenings in my life—past or present. In addition, I tended to record my therapeutic and hypnotic experiences. Sometimes it may have been one or two pages, but often it was as many as six. The material collected has helped in guiding me in the writing of this paper.

This is a journey of my past, the highs and lows, beginning with the legal entry of three Lopez brothers and their families into the United States in 1918, at which time I was not as yet born. Some material prior to my mother's death is primarily from hearsay or as told to me much later by relatives and family friends. Children from my generation, especially Hispanic children, were raised to not question the why and what of events, especially unusual ones. I realize that, unfortunately, at times I carried this expectation into adulthood. Perhaps I did a disservice to my children by unwittingly passing this part of my upbringing to them. Although my mother died when I was four years of age, few can refute, after reading this manuscript, that it was a major event that impacted her daughter Erminia's development deeply.

Unbeknownst to me at the time, a major task involved breaking and putting together painful events that resulted in how I came to be who I am today—that is, three personalities, pre her mother's death, post the death, and the resulting persona. The journey involved opening the door to repressed memories, putting them together, and dealing with them in order for healing to take effect. Often, breaking into the past has been accompanied by unshed, repressed tears as I wrote about traumatic incidences. At these times, I had need of a trusted friend, and it was my cousin Lupe Alvarez, living in San Antonio, to whom I turned. She was my uncle Benito's daughter. She listened without criticizing. She provided information on our family backgrounds and edited the material for punctuation and grammatical usage. After completing ten to twelve typed pages, I mailed them to her for her scrutiny. Once the corrections were made, the packet would be returned to me in the same large business envelope. This practice of using the same mailing envelope became a game. The same envelope to and from each other was used seven times. And we figured out a way to deal with addresses. To and from addresses were placed on top of another. When one party received a mailing, it was a matter of removing the top addresses. My friend Barb Roper, too, helped me by reviewing the completed manuscript and deleting words or phrases that were unnecessary and added nothing to the text. Thanks to her, the corrections made for better and smoother reading.

This is the struggle of an American Mexican, who in 1964, at the age of thirty-six and a mother of five, broke away from the barriers placed on her by Mexican and American culture to achieve her dream of attaining a much coveted goal—a college education. She dared enter the university arena, where, at the time of her entry, less than 1 percent of the population was of Hispanic heritage. The paper also addresses three major issues that I label as the "raping" of Minnie: (1) physical—the sexual molestation by Hispanic males and its devastating effect, (2) professional—the unwarranted probation by Anglos that, except for the memory of my mentor, could have broken my spirit, and (3) financially—the J. C. Reed fraud, the Anglos that fell short of bankrupting me, and, six months later, being scammed out of $11,000 cash by two perpetrators who spoke Spanish and looked Hispanic.

This American Mexican female was subjected to discrimination in grade school and high school, in housing, and possibly when seeking employment. But the encouragement and support for my efforts and to improve my life were received primarily from Anglos. The close friends I made along the way were Anglos. And two of these female friends and I have been friends for more than forty years; one was Barb, my next-door neighbor in Highland, and the other, Ann, I met at an agency. I have maintained a close relationship with many relatives, many of whom are not married to Hispanics.

My experience with the bilingual director, who apparently had no respect nor adequate training for the position for which he was hired, left me with the question as to whether it requires a Hispanic to deal with Hispanic problems. Apparently, this man, as evidenced by the mess in which he left his office, received inadequate training and possibly may have tailored his résumé for his purposes. His inappropriate behavior toward me indicated that he had little respect for women. This man's overall behavior did little to improve the image of minorities of Hispanic backgrounds.

As the reader will note, there have been many ups and downs in my life. I would be remiss if I did not cite the most precious blessings bestowed on me. In addition to my children, I have more than twenty-four grandchildren and great-grandchildren. At times when I am in need of a pick-me-up I reflect on the antics of some of the current little people in my life, my great-grandchildren, and the world brightens.

Behind some of the painful experiences I unwittingly faced was the trust and belief I had in people learned from the overall behavior of the Lopez brothers and being naïve. However painful, this journey was worth the undertaking-but it may not be for everyone!